THE FORMATIVE YEARS

The
FORMATIVE YEARS

Raising and Training
the Young Horse
from Birth to Two Years

by Cherry Hill

Photographs by Richard Klimesh

Breakthrough
Publications, Inc.

For information address:

Breakthrough Publications, Inc.
Millwood, New York 10546

International Standard Book Number: 0-914327-19-4
Library of Congress Catalog Card Number: 87-72003
Book design by Sheila Lynch

Printed in the United States of America

Reprinted 1993

Acknowledgments

Acknowledgment and thanks are given to the following individuals for assistance in editing various portions of this book: Richard Klimesh, Susan Dixon, Dale Forbes Bormann, Sally George, Todd Mowrer, and Dr. Robert K. Shideler.

Illustrations are by N.J. Wiley; photographs by Richard Klimesh and Cherry Hill.

Special thanks to the following photo models: Archer (Weanling), owned by Roland and Sue Dixon, handled by Sue Dixon; Isaac (Yearling), owned by Todd and Linda Mowrer, handled by Todd Mowrer; and Doctor Zip and Poconotion (Two-Year-Olds), both owned by Cherry Hill.

The horses in this book represent the following breeds: Arabian, Hanoverian, Oldenburg, Quarter Horse, Thoroughbred, and Trakehner.

To my mother (the artist) and
my father (the scientist) for
their encouragement
during *my* formative years.
And to Richard for his wonderful sense of life.

List of Illustrations

Contents

Preface

Placing a hand on a newborn foal is just as much a part of the training process as the first saddling. Whether the interactions are organized and deliberate or unplanned and casual, learning is taking place.

Quality rather than *quantity* of experience produces the best results with a young horse. A few well-designed lessons based on proven principles can promote a cooperative attitude, while tedious daily drilling may serve to develop resentment.

Training is replacing the horse's inborn fear of man's world with respect, trust, and a willingness to learn. The tactics for accomplishing these nonspecific goals depend in a large part on the particular disposition of the horse and the experience of the trainer.

Studying equine behavior will help the handler anticipate the probable outcome of various situations. Following a detailed, progressive training plan encourages desired responses from the horse, and helps to prevent unnecessary mistakes, problems, and accidents.

Because there has been very little equine behavioral research, the recommendations in this book are based on observation of many types, breeds, and ages of horses as they reacted to domestication and training situations.

Due to the deep affection between horses and man, horses are often viewed as if they have human characteristics. This anthropomorphic trap is dangerous for the handler and unfair to the horse. A horse is a horse.

I have chosen to refer to the horse with the male pronoun, except when specifically discussing the mare or the filly. The trainer/handler, on the other hand, is referred to as a female because the majority of horsemen today are actually horsewomen.

For convenience, in the training section additional necessary equipment is listed at the beginning of each chapter. Glossary terms appear in bold the first time they appear in the text.

It is my hope that the information in *The Formative Years* will be instrumental in helping you develop a successful personal training style. May your involvement be profitable and enjoyable!

Part One

BEHAVIOR
and
LEARNING

ONE

Evolution and the Nature of the Horse

For the past 60 million years, the horse has shown a superior ability to adapt to his environment. Predator avoidance and environmental demands forced physical changes upon prehistoric horses for survival.

In order to flee from his enemies, the horse developed an improved system of levers to move his body with quick reflexes and speed. A change to hinge joints in the lower legs made for more efficient movement. The decrease in the number of toes and the formation of a dense hoof allowed the horse to negotiate rough and varied terrain with speed. Elongated **nasal turbinates** increased air intake and warming capacity, which allowed the horse to flee faster, further, and in colder temperatures. In addition, the horse developed a long neck for more efficient grazing and improved balance. The grinding teeth became increasingly more dense, which aided in processing dry prairie grasses; the development of a **cecum** allowed the digestive system to increase its utilization of roughages.

Since domestication 5000 years ago, the horse has been required to live in man's world. Considering that the horse has been domesticated only a tiny fraction (1/12000) of the time since his species originated, his ability to adapt to man's demands is impressive. Today's **equus** acts much the same way his ancestors did, even though modern man may think the "wild" behavior is unnecessary. The horse is a **gregarious** nomad with a highly developed escape reflex.

SOCIALIZATION

Because horses desire companionship and derive security from each other, they are gregarious, or tend to live and move in groups. An example of this socialization is the strong dominance hierarchy within a herd. Horses are ranked in order according to authority. Factors affecting a horse's position include age, body size, strength, athletic ability, sex, length of time in a particular band or location, and **temperament**. Man is also a part of this **pecking order** and must establish himself indisputably as the top horse. Pecking order is usually exhibited most graphically at feeding time.

A social ritual practiced by horses is mutual grooming. Although the pairs of preferred associates are usually equally dominant, a timid horse can seek out a bold grooming partner and vice versa.

The social bonds between horses can become so strong that problems may occur. Separating certain individuals may cause panic or make a horse **barn sour** (or herd sour). Insecure horses ignore barriers and can be dangerous as they desperately try to return to their herdmates. Encouraging an independent attitude from an early age and developing a rapport between horse and trainer will help prevent these problems.

Foals socialize almost exclusively with their **dams** during the first several weeks following birth. If the situation allows, the month-old foal begins to spend increasingly longer periods away from his dam's side interacting with other foals. By perhaps two months of age, the foal begins to learn socially acceptable behavior with other foals' dams. And depending on the situation, he begins interaction and bonding with horses of various ages and sexes soon thereafter.

Ideally, socialization with man begins early but should not interfere with the necessary bonding to the dam. Handling of the foal may begin the second day but should not be overdone. Incorrect socialization or overhandling is worse than none at all. Strong negative emotions such as hunger, fear, pain, or loneliness tend to speed up the foal's socialization with humans but slow down learning. Strong positive emotions such as pride, well-being, and contentment tend to slow down the need for socialization, but set the stage for an increased rate of learning.

NOMADIC TENDENCIES

Horses are born wanderers. Often the distance between feeding or watering areas required extensive travel, so horses evolved by eating many small meals while continually on the move. With his muscles in motion and warmed up, his nerves ready to fire, and his senses keen, the horse in motion was most successful in detecting and escaping predators. Since horses are basically followers, the **nomadic** wanderings of a herd gave a horse a direction in which to move. Decisions were made by only a few individuals, namely the stallion and the lead mare.

THE FLIGHT REFLEX

Sharp senses and quick reactions have helped horses survive over millions of years. **Instincts** still prevail. When confronted with an imaginary or a real fear, horses seldom ask questions; instead they choose to flee. This escape reflex serves to demonstrate that horses are rarely aggressive unless cornered.

Shying, or demonstration of the startle response, can be an honest reaction to an object or situation, or a very irritating game. When encountering an unfamiliar or threatening object, many horses put a critical distance between themselves and the unknown. Ten feet might be sufficient for the initial inspection of a shirt on a rail, for example, but it might take a separation of one hundred feet for a horse to feel safe when first catching sight of a bouquet of balloons or an unfamiliar animal.

Sometimes the startle response can be explained by equine visual capabilities. Horses demonstrate the ability to perceive small moving objects at a greater distance than man. In addition, horses use both **monocular** and **binocular** vision. The binocular field spans about 60 to 70 degrees directly in front of the horse's face, where he focuses on one image with both eyes. In addition, each eye perceives a separate image in its own 135-degree monocular field. When an object moves from the binocular field to one of the monocular fields, the object may appear to jump or become distorted, and this can cause the horse concern. Blind spots exist directly behind the horse and immediately below his head, yet the total 340-degree field of his vision far exceeds that of man.

The horse's power of **adaptation** to various light intensities seems to operate more slowly than man's, as evidenced by a horse's behavior as he emerges from a dark barn into the bright sunlight or as he approaches a dark trailer in the bright sunlight. It is thought, however, that the range of adaptation, although slower, is actually wider in horses than man. Certain physiological features of the horse's eye occlude excess sunlight, while others reflect and intensify rays in low-light situations.

It has long been disputed just how a horse focuses on near or distant objects and how his visual power of **accommodation** compares to that of man. It appears that horses must raise their heads to see far-off objects and lower them when inspecting something close up. Owing to the shape of the eyeball and construction of the lens and ciliary muscles, it is thought that the **acuity** of a horse's vision is less than that of man.

TEMPERAMENT

Temperament is the general consistency with which a horse behaves. Temporary attitude changes may be caused by specific conditions, but the basic personality of a horse remains constant. Many factors contribute to a horse's temperament. Some are inherent at birth while others result from early experiences and the environment.

Genetic influences on temperament include type, breed, and family lines. Through selection at breeding time, **hot-blooded** or **cold-blooded** traits are perpetuated. These can be reflected in hair coat, bone size, and breed characteristics as well as in temperament factors such as sensitivity, athletic potential, and level-headedness.

The sex of a horse and the subsequent hormone levels often affect his (or her) behavioral patterns. In addition, certain conformational traits can have a large effect on temperament. The physiology of the senses, for example, can contribute to or undermine a horse's security. Horses with large, prominent eyes have a wider field of vision than do those with small, "pig" eyes.

Other physical factors that affect temperament are age, health, physical condition, and diet. These are most often governed by the environment, or in the case of domestication, the management provided by the animal's owner.

Early experiences with man and other horses have a lasting effect on the personality of a young horse. Horses need to learn acceptable limits of social behavior within the herd hierarchy. If they are sheltered from interaction when young, they often do not act wisely when it later becomes necessary to socialize with other horses. It is important to let a horse be a horse.

The development of an improper relationship with humans or too much socialization with a handler can be disorienting for a horse. Confusion only leads to mistakes in judgment on the parts both of the trainer and of the horse. It is best if the roles are made clear. Even a horse with a wonderful temperament can be ruined by inconsistent or conflicting treatment.

When choosing a horse, it is paramount to select one with a cooperative attitude. Whether a sensitive or a tolerant character would be most suitable for you depends on your competence and your planned use for the horse. Sensitivity can easily be misinterpreted as disobedience if a horse reacts quickly to a **cue** or overreacts to a cue of improper intensity. A tolerant horse will better withstand handler error and may accept more variations of a particular cue without becoming confused. While the tolerant horse may not become the brilliant performer that the sensitive horse does, he may be better insulated against imperfections in training techniques and would be more appropriate for a first-time training project.

Training a horse with an uncooperative attitude is difficult but not impossible. Making such a horse want to work is a challenge; you will need to preserve the horse's good opinion of himself so that lessons are enjoyable.

Probably the toughest type of horse to train is the uncooperative, insensitive horse. Not only does he avoid work, but he is also physically unresponsive to cues. This is a frustrating type of horse even for a professional, and is generally inappropriate for a novice. An uncooperative, hypersensitive horse is also a dangerous combination. Training a thin-skinned horse with a mental attitude that says "Make me!" can lead to frequent and dangerous blowups.

Horses that are intolerant characteristically perform their work with a grudge: ears back, tails swishing, unforgiving of a new trainer. Not only are these unsuitable horses to use for lessons, they are also less pleasurable to train. When selecting a horse, choose a sound individual with a good mind. A flashy coat and a few extra inches in height should be viewed as an added bonus rather than the criteria for selection.

COMMUNICATION

A horse communicates primarily with expressions and movements. Vocalization is secondary. Because body language is the main means a horse has of conveying feelings and intentions, it behooves the horse trainer to recognize and use it appropriately in her own actions.

A horse's eyes, ears, teeth, mouth, and nostrils convey information about his health and mental state. Pinched nostrils, ears at half mast, and dull eyes can indicate both illness and sullenness. With experience you can learn to tell the difference. The message behind bared teeth is unmistakable, but ears back can mean either that a kick is coming or that the horse is concentrating very hard on his work.

Smell is the horse's primary recognition tool and the ritual is to smell without being smelled. Once two horses have formed a bond, however, the smelling process is brief and nonthreatening. Although it is tempting to pet the soft portion of a horse's nose, doing so violates the horse's sensitive tactile and olfactory apparatus. In addition, dabbing at the nose can encourage nibbling. Horses, especially the curious youngsters, use their sense of smell to become familiar with their trainer and equipment. Oily surfaces tend to carry more of a characteristic scent, so horses investigate the trainer's ears, nose, and hair for information. Between horses, the scent-recognition ritual is often followed by mutual grooming. To avoid having your neck or back nibbled, be aware that nibbling often follows sniffing and be ready to discourage it.

Signs that precede an aggressive act include swishing the tail, lifting a hind leg, lowering the croup, laying the ears back, and lowering the head and neck. However, the same movements can also indicate pain from colic.

Even though vocalization is a secondary form of communication for horses, they do have a wide range of sounds that indicate various emotions. The frantic screams of a weanling, the squeals of a teasing mare, the snorts of a proud stallion, the whinny of a hungry horse, the groan of the performance horse turned out to roll after a work, the affectionate nicker of a dam to her foal, and many others sounds are further clues to the feelings of a horse.

DAILY ROUTINES

The horse is a creature of habit with a strong biological clock. He is most content when allowed to order his day according to his instincts and needs. Although wild horses have been observed to stick rather closely to definite daily patterns, seasonal variations occur as do daily changes determined by the weather, temperature, air flow, humidity, and atmospheric pressure. Horses tend to be restless in the wind, lethargic in high humidity, and unpredictable when the barometer is changing.

The most important routine from the horse's point of view is eating. As previously mentioned, the horse evolved as a nomadic grazer, and he prefers small, frequent meals. Feeding once a day is totally inappropriate, especially for young horses. Foals, because of their small stomachs, may nurse every half hour for the first few weeks of their life. As their stomach capacity increases, so do the periods they can go between meals. Left to their own choices, pastured horses will leisurely graze for a large part of their waking hours. Confined horses look forward to their meals on time and can become noisy and upset if feedings are missed or late.

Most horses drink water at a specific time of day, usually after ingestion of roughages. No matter how convincing the handler might try to be, it is nearly impossible to force a horse to drink off schedule. Having fresh water available at all times is the best insurance that a horse will be able to satisfy his thirst when he is ready.

Many horses, even those in confinement, choose particular places to deposit their feces. In large pastures, horses usually use separate areas for eating and elimination. This is a natural means of parasite control. Reinfestation will occur daily if horses are forced to eat in an area of fecal contamination. Horses defecate from five to twelve times per day. Each bowel movement consists of five to twenty fecal balls, and each fecal ball can contain as many as 30,000 parasite eggs. Therefore, it is wise to make arrangements for sanitary feeding.

Horses experience different types of rest in the three sleep positions: standing, sternal recumbent, and **lateral** recumbent. The standing position is commonly observed when the horse is dozing on three legs with the stay apparatus and check ligaments locking his front legs into a rigid stance. Yearlings and older horses may spend as many as four of their seven resting hours in this position.

Slow-wave sleep is generally achieved when the horse is in the sternal recumbent position. In this position the horse lies with his legs folded under him and his head lowered or even with the muzzle resting on the ground. About two of the seven hours a horse rests are spent in this position.

The lateral recumbent position is characteristic of deep sleep. The horse lies flat on the ground on one side with legs extended. Often the horse is observed to whinny, run, or twitch in this paradoxical sleep. If environmental conditions allow, a horse will sleep in this manner for one of the seven rest hours per day.

Although wild horses almost always sleep during the day in order to keep vigil for predators at night, domestic horses sleep during both day and night. Foals, especially during their first few weeks, spend the majority of their time eating and sleeping. The healthy foal will most commonly be observed in the sternal recumbent or lateral recumbent position. By the time a horse is two, he forms a close approximation to his adult habits.

Play is essential behavior for both the physical and social development of foals. It is best if young horses are allowed to play with horses their own age. Older horses aren't interested in the same games and many are impatient with a foal's vitality.

Play teaches a foal fighting behavior, sets the stage for sexual training, sharpens reflexes, develops the competitive spirit, and improves overall stamina. Foals begin to test their limits in their first month and continue these antics as long as they have an interested playmate. If a young horse has had inadequate exercise and socialization, he may attempt to play with the trainer during lessons.

Horses perform various grooming rituals on a regular basis. Self-grooming includes rolling, rubbing, and nibbling and is heightened in intensity during shedding and muddy months. Horses roll on the ground to scratch themselves, remove loose hair, counteract the plastering effect of rain, loosen sweat, and coat themselves with a layer of mud to ward off insects. Rather than preventing a young horse from fulfilling this natural desire, it is better to control where he rolls. Turning a horse out after a lesson for half an hour in a sand pen will allow him to perform his ritual at the same time he cools and dries for better grooming.

For both companionship and physical pleasure, horses form grooming partnerships and nibble each other on the areas that would be hard to reach alone. This mutual grooming usually starts with two horses smelling each other and then assuming a position which allows one horse to scratch the other's withers. Working their way down the backbone, these preferred associates provide a valuable service to each other.

PRESSURES OF DOMESTICATION

Today's horses are often subjected to extended confinement and a demand to adapt to man's schedule. If a horse owner does not fully understand the nature of the horse, she may subject her animals to conditions that are so unnatural that the horse has difficulty being comfortable mentally and physically.

Horses that are unable to adapt to their environment often develop behavior abnormalities that are a direct result of conflict, uncertainty, or restriction. Conflict occurs when the horse has two opposing urges, both equally strong. Uncertainty results when the horse is faced with a problem beyond his power of resolution. Restriction comes when a horse is limited in his movement during training or is confined in a stable.

Two categories of behavior abnormalities that horses can form are **vices** and bad habits. Vices are reactions to life in the stable and include wood chewing, pawing, tail rubbing, weaving, pacing, and kicking the stall. Most vices are best prevented and treated by attention to proper diet, exercise, and socialization. Bad habits are responses to improper handling and training. Rearing, pulling, biting, and striking are undesirable behaviors exhibited by the horse who feels rushed, threatened, or confused in his training.

TWO

Maturity and Learning

The foal is born with needs equivalent to a human infant's: he is preoccupied with hunger, thirst, sleep, and comfort. However, within hours of birth, the foal has the physical ability and mechanical skills of a two-year-old human. Twenty-four hours after birth the foal is able to run, using legs that are 90 percent of the length of an adult horse's. Coupled with keen instincts, this physical advantage has helped the young horse survive over the millennia. However, sometimes this strength and energy is expressed too exuberantly and foals overstress themselves, especially when they are turned out following extended confinement. In spite of their apparent vigor, foals are fragile, both mentally and physically, and need close contact and security from their dam.

The suckling foal is characteristically inquisitive yet timid, fractious yet vulnerable, feisty yet fearful. Although it is advantageous to handle the youngster before he gets unwieldy, you should make the sessions short, firm, fair, and to the point.

By weaning time at four to six months of age, the horse has reached the human physical equivalent of about a four to five-year-old child and the emotional equivalent of a two to three-year-old. With a short attention span and a tendency toward unpredictable outbursts, weanlings are best left to be horses. Necessary lessons should be kept safe and fun.

The weanling is very impressionable and can experience deep emotional and physical trauma. Care must be taken to preserve his interest in eating and other routines so that he does not become unnecessarily depressed. The young horse separated from his mother is uncertain about his safety. In addition, he is required to form his own behavior patterns for the first time.

The yearling spends much of his time experimenting with his

skills and finding his place in equine and human society. The equivalent emotionally of a five-year-old human and physically of an eight-year-old, the yearling horse is testy, and can be rambunctious or moody. Fillies and colts are beginning to experience the effects of the hormones of puberty, and sexually oriented games are incorporated into playtime.

Approximate Human Equivalents to Young Horses

Horse's Age	Physical Equivalent	Emotional Equivalent	Comments
Birth	2-year-old (Infant)	Newborn	Mechanical skills: Legs = survival
4 months	4-year-old (Toddler)	2-year-old	Play; weaning
6 months	5-year-old (Kindergartner)	3-year-old	Impressionable; frisky; sex play; short attention span
1 year	8-year-old (Pre-adolescent)	5-year-old	**Gelding**/Estrous; testy, moody
2-year-old	15-year-old (Adolescent)	8-year-old	Joints mature; serious sex drive

It is imperative that the lessons started with a foal be thoroughly reviewed with the yearling. Although sessions should still be short, they can be more frequent and cover a wider variety of handling. The yearling is receptive and capable of learning all of the ground rules.

With the two-year-old year comes serious sex drive and its subsequent effect on attention during training. Although only the physical equivalent of a fourteen to fifteen-year-old human and the mental equivalent of an eight-year-old, the two-year-old horse is too often treated as a mature horse.

Many of the **epiphyseal** closures in the two-year-old's joints will have matured, but he should not be made to accept the work load of an adult. He lacks the stamina and strength to perform under a rigorous schedule. His skeletal immaturity also leaves him prone to injury. Having lost much of his yearling silliness the two-year-old generally pays attention, and you can guage his potential.

LEARNING

Horses are not ranked very highly as problem solvers, but they are respected for their keen **power of association** and adaptability. Using brain size as an indicator of **intelligence,** horses have been referred to as dumb beasts. While man's brain comprises 2.5 percent of his body weight, the horse's brain is a mere .13 percent of his mass.

With a natural ability to link a stimulus with a response, the horse's power of association is very strong. Aided by a memory often said to be second only to an elephant's, the horse rarely forgets lessons—good or bad. Although this can be a boon for the successful trainer, it can be the downfall for a novice who may make many mistakes on the first horse she trains. Whether or not the handler views an interaction with a horse as a formal training session or not, the horse is always learning.

Once a horse has learned a lesson, you may find his anticipation troublesome. Before you even present the cues, your horse may begin to perform what he expects will be asked. A particular obstacle, a place in the arena, or your body language may give him the clue. Although anticipation may seem harmless or novel at first, it can develop into a habit that can make a horse virtually uncontrollable. To prevent anticipation, you should vary the sequence of your maneuvers and the location of your lessons and keep the lessons moving forward in a progressive fashion.

Horses remember past associations for years and with alarming clarity. A cute pony foal who has been taught to put his front legs on the shoulders of his owner to amuse visitors will remember the lesson in spite of his 600-pound weight when he is five years old.

The first type of learning that a foal experiences is **imprinting**. This is the process of dam and species bonding that takes place during the first few hours after birth. The odors of the placental fluids and the sounds exchanged between foal and dam create innate behaviors in the foal. Human interference too soon after foaling can cause long-lasting disorientation in the foal. Some youngsters inadvertently imprinted with human smells and sounds have trouble locating their dam, or worse yet, experience difficulty relating to their species in general.

Modeling or mimicking the behavior of other horses takes place in herds as well as in training situations. Young horses who observe successful **longeing** or riding sessions are less likely to be alarmed by the process when it is their turn.

Trainers use the principles of **habituation** or flooding when they want their horses to accept a certain procedure or object without fear. "Gentling" or **"sacking out"** a horse with blankets and slickers is a way of gradually decreasing his apprehensions concerning an object. By repeated exposure to a certain stimulus, a horse usually has a diminished response to it.

Sometimes a horse has been taught a lesson but has not exhibited to the trainer that he has learned it. After a few days off, the horse performs the lessons perfectly. This is **latent** learning and is commonly observed in horses.

BEHAVIOR MODIFICATION

A horse is always exhibiting some sort of behavior. Through behavior modification, you can mold the horse's actions into a useful format. When the horse behaves consistently with your desires and you want to encourage him to repeat such behavior in the future, you need to reinforce that behavior. When his behavior is undesirable, you should discourage that behavior and show him a different way to act. Then positively reinforce the new behavior.

Whether you use positive or negative reinforcement, it should be immediate, consistent, appropriate, and concise. A good trainer is an objective observer, only noting actual behaviors, not her interpretations of a horse's actions. Assigning a numerical score or grade to variants in a horse's behavior and recording them is a good way to develop a sense of observation. Ranking a horse's **trot** work on the longe line using a 1-to-10 scale will help you objectively evaluate improvement. Remarks such as "It was brilliant," or "He was really trying," add color but are quite subjective.

There are four ways to modify or reinforce behavior: **positive reinforcement, punishment, extinction,** and **negative reinforcement**. Rewarding a horse for good behavior by attempting to make him feel good is positive reinforcement. This encourages the horse to repeat the behavior in the future. Although not always recommended for routine training situations, feeding a horse a treat is an example of a reward. Horses can also learn to appreciate a kind word or a pat on the neck as a reward. These kinds of positive reinforcements are much more convenient for everyday horse training.

When we discipline a horse to discourage a certain behavior, we are punishing him. Sometimes all that is necessary is a verbal reprimand, but often physical discipline is needed to make a lasting impression on a horse. If a yearling refuses to stop when you are leading him, you may have to resort to a chain over his nose so that when he fails to respond to your request for a halt, you can apply pressure on the chain. As you discipline the horse with the chain, use a **voice command** simultaneously; eventually the voice command alone will produce the same results. Physical punishment is automatically administered by an electric fence. When a horse misbehaves by leaning over the fence, he is shocked and subsequently discouraged from repeating that behavior.

Removing a negative stimulus once a horse has performed the behavior you desire is termed negative reinforcement. When teaching a young horse to move over while tied, you must teach him to move away from pressure at his ribs. Using a finger or other object, you will tap the horse in the ribs until he takes a step sideways; his reward is the escape from the pressure. Each time it will take fewer jabs to get him moving sideways. Soon just a light fingertip will guide him. He has been trained by negative reinforcement. This particular lesson will carry over to the first time a rider asks for the horse to yield to the leg. Pressure is applied and repeated with boot and/or spur until the horse moves away from the leg.

Extinction is the removal of something pleasant to discourage the behavior it follows. Unfortunately, a horse that whinnies noisily at feeding time gets a reward for his obnoxious behavior every time he gets fed. To stop this habit, you should not feed the horse when he is noisy, but wait until he is quiet and then give him the feed. With extinction, the animal's undesirable behavior usually becomes greatly amplified and embellished before it diminishes. The horse will whinny louder and louder and may add stamping, snorting, and pawing to his routine. Understandably, many people relent when the behavior is at its worst, but it is precisely then that the behavior is about to disappear. After a few rewards for being silent, the horse will begin to associate quiet behavior with feeding time.

SHAPING

Once your horse has linked a particular set of **aids** to the maneuver being requested, you should begin to ask for a gradual improvement in form. This is called **shaping** or reinforcing successive approximations to a desired behavior.

When first teaching the tiny foal to lead, you teach him that a tug on the noseband of his halter impedes his forward motion. Your eventual goal is to have the foal stop squarely alongside you when you give a light tug on the lead rope. Getting to that stage takes a series of steps that span several lessons. The foal must be rewarded each time he gets closer to the final goal.

When first teaching the two-year-old to **canter** on the longe line, you should accept just about anything that leads to a canter without bucking or pulling. You should then gradually hone the **transition** until the horse will not only canter from a trot or a **walk**, but will do so with proper balance, rhythm, and **engagement**. Reaching the goal is a progression that takes time. You must reward the horse for his improvement along the way.

When shaping your horse's behavior, remember the following principles: Start with the best base, reward all approximations to the desired behavior, don't move too fast toward the goal, and don't get stuck in one particular stage.

- **Start with best base.** In the preceding examples, the foal is more likely to understand what you want if the first time you tug on his halter and say "Whoa" he wanted to stop anyway. Having someone lead the dam and stop her should provide the necessary incentive for the foal to want to stop. It would not be productive to take the foal away from its mother for the first lesson; a frantic, anxious youngster is not a receptive student.

    The two-year-old would understand your intentions most clearly if the first time you asked for a canter he was fresh and ready to move on. It is also helpful to use a crisp voice command and assertive body language.

- **Reward all approximations to the desired behavior.** Release of the pressure on the foal's lead rope when he stops is a reward. Letting the foal stop by his mother's side is a reward. Soon the foal can learn that a pat or kind word is a reward.

  If the two-year-old bolts into a canter and begins running, the trainer must remain calm and praise the horse for his attempt. Even if the young horse takes the wrong **lead**, it is usually best to reward him for the cantering before you try again for a particular lead. Soon the horse will relax and the correct response will come easily.

- **Don't move too fast toward the goal.** If you try to reach perfection in just a few sessions, your horse may miss valuable connections between the lesson's components. The beauty of a systematic training scheme is that when you have problems, you always have a progression that can be reviewed.

- **Don't get stuck in one particular stage.** If you are approaching the ultimate goal and no longer gear the lessons to forward progress, advancing the horse's behavior could be more difficult. For example, if the foal is led behind the dam for four months, it will be difficult to convince him that he can operate independently. If for the first three months of longeing, the two-year-old is allowed one or two trot strides in between a transition from walk to canter, it will be difficult to erase them. Keeping the lessons progressing will yield maximum performance and satisfaction.

Part Two

TRAINING

THREE

Training Principles
and Guidelines

The goal of horse handling is to bend the horse rather than break him. Presenting the horse with progressive, well-planned lessons that alter his behavior in subtle ways is the art of horse training.

A horse is much more secure if his role is made perfectly clear. It is often difficult for the horse-lover to administer the discipline necessary for effective training; however it is essential to show the horse the boundaries within which he must work. Horses do not initially know the difference between our definitions of "good" and "bad." Being creatures of habit, they will always be forming behavior patterns. No matter what you are doing with your horse, he is being trained. Therefore, when planning a training session, you should try to have a very specific order of events in mind. Although it helps to be flexible within the preestablished plan, you should set a goal for each training session.

Distractions prevent the horse in training from giving his full attention to the lesson. For example, it is best to eliminate dogs from the arena, postpone lawn mowing, and reschedule the turnout of rambunctious weanlings in the adjacent pasture if you plan to work with a horse that is very young or inexperienced. Of course the horse should eventually perform regardless of external conditions; but initially, the young horse needs no distractions from his concentration.

Assigning one trainer to a horse reduces the chance for confusion from conflicting or slightly different signals. Later, once the horse has become steady in his responses, it is wise to begin exposing him to a variety of competent handlers so that he develops a tolerance for variance.

It is counterproductive to rush during a training session. You should take time to move through the progressive steps of a maneuver. Teaching the horse one thing at a time is only fair. Your movements around the horse should be smooth, but not necessarily slow.

The successful trainer expects the best from each training session, but is prepared for the worst. With a positive **attitude**, approach the training arena with the appropriate equipment and with safety in mind. Playing the "worst case scenario" out in your mind ahead of time will help you visualize how to react if things do go wrong.

A good horse trainer is objective in her observations. Rather than recording or stating interpretations of behavior, it is more helpful in the long run to stick to the facts. Instead of saying a horse is angry, describe his behavior by the action of his tail or the position of his ears.

Horses interpret what is actually happening, not the intentions of the handler. So remember, even if you are doing something for the horse's own good (walking toward him with a syringe of penicillin, for example), he may see it quite differently.

Horses move away from light **intermittent pressure** and into heavy, steady pressure. If you've ever tried to move an untrained horse over and resorted to leaning your body into him, you most likely found that the horse leaned into you with all of his weight. As odd as it might seem, a light tap or pesky little tickle on the ribs is more effective in making a horse move away than constant pressure. Take a lesson from how horses react to flies. Touch is an active sense, not static. Prolonged or repeated touch desensitizes a horse. When communicating with the horse, whether through a halter or with your hand, small jerks and taps are much more effective than an all-out tug of war.

Always use the least amount of force or punishment necessary to get the job done. This will not only leave you several "aces in the hole," but it also assures that the horse is being treated fairly and humanely. It is important, however, to use enough force to get the job done.

Reinforcement of a behavior must be administered immediately, otherwise you will be rewarding a different behavior. Two seconds is a subjective rule. If your horse bites you when you are turning him loose it would make no sense to catch him and punish him. He would then be being punished for getting caught. If your timing is inopportune to punish (or reward), set the stage to repeat the behavior. "Bait" the horse to repeat his mistake and then be ready with a quick response.

When beginning a training session, always start with a lesson the horse knows very well. This prepares him mentally and physically for the more difficult, new work, which should be presented in the middle of the session. End on a positive note with an activity the horse enjoys doing that allows him to cool down mentally and physically.

For a weanling a session might entail grooming for ten minutes, fifteen minutes of in-hand work, and five minutes of grooming. The two-year-old may be expected to warm up with some in-hand work, learn the basics of **ground-driving** in a twenty-minute lesson, and have five minutes of grooming at the end. An approximate schedule follows.

Approximate Lengths of Sessions for the Young Horse

Age	Length of Sessions	Frequency of Sessions
Foal	15 minutes	3 times per week
Weanling	30 minutes	3 times per week
Yearling	30-60 minutes	3 times per week
2-Year-Old	60 minutes	3 times per week

If there is a problem that requires immediate attention, such as preparation for farrier care or haltering a hard-to-catch horse, schedule the lessons on a daily basis until progress is made. It may be necessary to work a particular youngster more intensely than the above schedule for a month and then not handle him at all for several months. It depends on what needs to be accomplished and whether the horse is making progress.

BODY LANGUAGE AND VOICE COMMANDS

Since horses communicate primarily by nonvocal means, they expect the same mode of expression in their interaction with humans. The body language of the trainer indicates confidence, strength, and specific expectations of the horse. Since horses are insecure followers, they are willing to take the guidance of a handler who walks with sure steps, moves in smooth movements, and whose heartbeat and breathing are steady and calm.

There are training situations where you must be assertive and others where a passive, nonthreatening manner is more appropriate and productive. Your body stance and movements will indicate to the horse whether he should be afraid, attentive, or relaxed.

Every trainer possesses four natural aids: the mind, the hands, the voice, and the body. (The body is usually referred to as the legs, seat, and back when riding.) In addition, you can utilize artificial aids such as a longeing whip, which encourages forward movement as a rider's legs would, or a chain lead **shank**, which intensifies the action of the hand. However, artificial aids should not supersede a good understanding and use of the natural aids. Your strongest asset is your mind. A good trainer of young horses learns through trial and error the appropriate choreography of body language. The proper coordination of the body parts into harmonious gestures can make ground training appear easy.

In conjunction with body language, you should introduce voice commands. Horses quickly make an association between physical and verbal cues. Then, when necessary, you can rely on the verbal cues to elicit behavior. It is important, however, to follow a pattern with the commands to prevent confusion.

Voice commands must be consistent in the word used, the pitch, the inflection, and the volume. Selection of the word for a command is more meaningful for the human than for the horse. We traditionally use "Whoa" or "Ho" to command a horse to stop, but we could use "Bup!" instead. To the horse, any word is perfectly fine as long as it is consistent and has onomatopoeic potential (imitates the natural sound of the action). However, learning a traditional word can help a horse in understanding the commands of future trainers.

The pitch, or musical tone, of your voice gives the horse a big clue to the meaning of the command. Chirping the trot command in high tones encourages a horse to move forward, while a deep bass voice is more convincing for a "Whoa." When a mother tells her baby in loving sing-song tones that he is such a stinker, it is the tone of her voice that makes him laugh and coo, not the words she says. So it is with horses. Let the tone of your voice make a statement of your mood and intentions.

Connected closely with pitch is inflection or modulation: the rise and fall of the voice. A rising inflection tends to make a horse move forward and a falling inflection to slow or settle.

It is best to vary the word sounds in your horse's repertoire. If you try to include both "Whoa" and "No" in his vocabulary, the horse is likely to stop when you say "No," even though you may have intended the command to deter another behavior. The foal needs to learn "Walk on," "Trot," and "Whoa." Later lessons will require "Back," "Canter," "Turn," and any number of specialized commands.

The horse's sense of hearing enables him to hear very quiet tones. It is unnecessary to scream or shout commands. The "breaking patter" used by some trainers is just a rhythmic string of melodic words spoken at low volume to soothe and reassure the young horse.

REFLEXES

Reflexes are automatic, unconscious responses of a muscle to certain stimuli. Natural selection favored horses who escaped their predators. These individuals passed along their highly developed instincts, and today's horses exhibit a vast array of deeply ingrained reflex chains. Because reflexes are unconscious reactions, they can be a potential danger. A horse does not think before responding; it is done automatically. Fortunately, it is possible to override these instincts and train the horse not to respond reflexively in certain situations.

If a very young foal is nibbled by his dam or scratched by a human at the top of his tail, it causes the foal to suck, and he will search for his dam's udder. Often, any rubbing along the spinal column, such as when two horses perform mutual grooming, will precipitate oral movement. The human groom needs to override the young horse's desire to orally reciprocate. Nuzzling and nibbling lead to biting. A prompt, firm slap coupled with a voice command such as "Stop!" is usually an effective deterrent.

The withdrawal reflex causes the horse to snap his leg off the ground when it is touched by a fly or a hand or clippers. Certainly you want to preserve your horse's natural protective instincts, but you also want to work safely around his legs. You must train the horse to keep his weight on the leg for clipping, grooming, and bandaging.

The croup and perineal reflex chains cause a horse to clamp his tail, tuck his croup, and possibly kick and buck when the underside of the tail or the anus is touched, especially with something cold such as a neoprene tail wrap or water. This is an automatic physical response to attack, to the unfamiliarity of **tack**, or to handling.

The *cutaneous trunci* chain is responsible for the rapid and repeated contraction of the skin over the horse's barrel when a fly lands on his rib cage, for example. It is the same reflex that may make a horse hypersensitive to leg cues.

The *spina prominens* chain causes a horse to hollow his back if you run a fingernail down his spine. Improper **conditioning** or ill-fitting tack coupled with this reflex may lead to bucking when the horse is saddled or ridden.

If you are aware of the origin and nature of reflex chains, you can design systematic lessons to rid the horse of his fears and to override the reflexes.

SAFETY

Handling young horses can be surprisingly dangerous. Owing to the handler's vulnerable position, the unpredictable outbursts of young horses, and the nature of the equipment necessary for ground training, things can get in a tangle in a hurry.

As a safeguard, always carry a sharp pocketknife in case the only way out of a dilemma is to cut ropes. Even though you may use quick-release knots and **panic snaps**, there are times when the weight of a struggling horse may prevent these safety devices from operating.

Because so much ground training involves ropes and long lines, it is imperative that you become accustomed to wearing gloves for protection against rope burn. Never wrap or loop a rope around your hand, arm, or other part of your body. You should wear boots or durable shoes to protect your feet from the frequent missteps a young horse makes as he learns his boundaries.

Use equipment of the strongest type and periodically inspect it for wear as added insurance that the young horse will not learn bad habits. If he should escape a lesson by breaking a piece of weak equipment it could set the stage for a lifelong habit of attempting to repeat the scenario.

Tack should be well stitched and constructed from durable materials that are not fatigued from sweat, weather, or dirt. The hardware should be of the highest quality affordable and you should inspect the assembly for appropriate design. Some tack is colorful and attractive but may not be reliable under severe stress.

Training facilities need to be constructed for safety and strength. Horses should only be tied to very stout posts. It only takes one experience with breaking a rail and dragging the fragmented piece behind in a frenzy to give a horse a phobia about being tied. A horse's power and unpredictability are often underestimated. Working a horse in an enclosure with flimsy fences is asking for trouble. The first time the horse is pressured into accepting your rules, he may take out a section of fence and in the process injure himself and others.

The footing for training young horses should ideally be the same as the surface they are to be worked on as adults. If the horses are geared for arena competition, a round pen with a four to six-inch base of sand will be fine for longeing and driving. Although an endurance prospect could benefit from pony lessons on the terrain that he will encounter as an adult, working an unbalanced and/or unshod young horse in uneven, rocky, or slippery terrain can be dangerous. Until the youngster gains some experience and conditioning, you should hold the training sessions in a level area that provides adequate cushion.

FOUR

The Suckling Foal

CATCHING AND HALTERING

Equipment: The nylon halter must be well-fitted and strong. If working with a two-day-old foal, you need to purchase a suckling halter that can be adjusted to fit his tiny head. Doubled and stitched nylon-web halters with solid brass buckles and hardware are the sturdiest. In order to properly fit the newborn foal, however, you may find a soft rope halter offers more adjustment (photo 1). Leather halters are acceptable for in-hand work, but should never be used when tying.

The lead rope should be ¾-inch cotton rope with a finished length of about ten feet (photo 2). A heavy, well-made bull snap should be braided into one end. Beware of cheap cast snaps; they snap in more ways than one. The other end of the rope should be tied in a **crown knot**, then **back-spliced** and **whipped**.

Catching

There are generally three reasons that horses are difficult to catch: fear, resentment, or habit. A young horse must overcome his fear of human movements and touch before he will feel safe being restrained by his handler. Older horses may avoid being caught and haltered because they resent the treatment they get after being caught. Excessively hard work, ill-fitting gear, painful doctoring, or abuse can all cause **evasion** on the horse's part.

Once a horse has successfully avoided being caught several times, he may merely act out of habit. Perhaps there is no longer an unpleasant condition that can be blamed for the behavior, but the horse still shuns the handler. It may even turn into a game that the horse enjoys playing.

For whatever reason, whether teaching a young horse about being caught and haltered or retraining an older horse, my favorite method is the "walk-down method." Ideally, you should gently but firmly cradle the two-day-old foal in your arms, teaching him to submit and not to fear (photo 3). Have an assistant hold the dam the first several times you catch the foal. When approaching the foal, be nonthreatening in your body language and aim directly at

1. A strong halter capable of various adjustments is necessary for the suckling foal.

2. A ten-foot cotton lead rope.

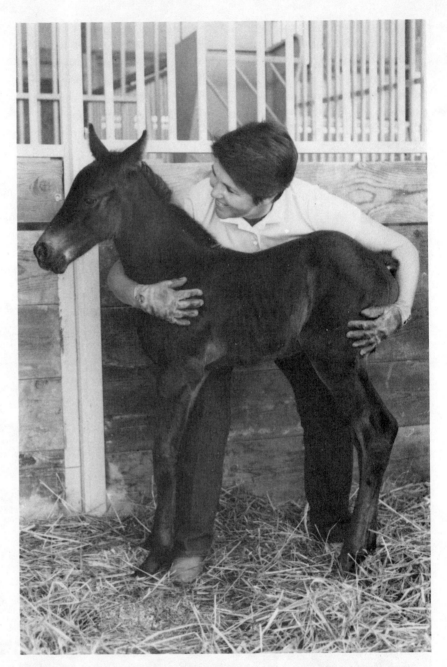

3. The two-day-old foal is held firmly with much body-to-body contact.

the side of the young horse. If you approach from behind it encourages the youngster to scoot forward, and approaching his head can make him wheel. If you keep a position at the middle of the foal's body, you can embrace the foal from fore to aft: on the near (left) side, for example, it would be left arm at the chest and right arm behind the buttocks. Gentle but firm body-to-body contact usually convinces the foal that struggling is not necessary. A tenuous grip may encourage the foal to experiment with the boundaries of his first **restraint**.

Once the foal is accustomed to being caught in a box stall, it is time to move the lesson to a small pen. This is where the walk-down method really begins. The rules are:

1. Always walk toward the horse's shoulder, never toward his rump or head.

2. Never move faster than a walk.

3. Always be the first to turn and walk away from the foal.

Don't be in a hurry the first time you try this technique; it may be quite some time before the young horse gives up and turns to face what is pursuing him. At first, all you do is approach the youngster, scratch him in the area of his withers, then turn and walk away. Because nothing frightening has happened, the foal is less reluctant to let a human approach the next time. After a few times of scratching and walking away, you should actually catch the foal and cradle him in your arms for a minute before turning him loose. If it took twenty minutes for you to approach the foal the first time, perhaps it will only take ten the second, two the third, and soon just a few seconds. The dam can be held by an assistant for the first few lessons, but eventually the foal will allow himself to be caught regardless of the situation. This is the beginning of building a young horse's aptitude for independence.

Progress with the walk-down method to larger and larger pens until you can approach the foal in the pasture without him fleeing. Based on repetition and lack of trauma, this method is worth the time and effort it takes as it instills good habits in a horse for years to come.

There are quicker methods of catching, and in some instances they may be necessary. Cornering a young horse in a safe pen is usually a job for two or three knowledgeable people. When confined, young horses can be unpredictable and may try to leap fences or people in an attempt to get away. Some horses give in when they see two or more people approach, but are very testy if a single person enters their pen. This type would benefit from a thorough walk-down regimen.

The natural tendency of a cornered horse is to turn his hindquarters to danger. If a horse is unsure of humans, he will behave this way as a defensive measure. The principle behind whip-breaking a horse is to get him to turn around and face you by whipping him on the hock or rump. Of course, this method is very dangerous since whipping a cornered horse can cause him to jump over the walls of the enclosure, whirl and lunge past you, or, perhaps most dangerously, kick out with both hind feet in reflex. It is not a recommended procedure for any but the most experienced trainers. However, since many young horses will try to avoid being caught by turning their rumps to the handler, it is beneficial if the handler understands the principles involved.

When a horse presents his rump you have two choices: to go into the corner and risk getting kicked or having the horse whirl away or to make the horse turn around and face you. You can usually get a foal to face you by slapping him with your hand or giving him a little pop with the end of the lead rope on the top of the croup. Used judiciously, this startling act makes the youngster turn and face you, at which point you should say, "Good boy (or girl)" in soothing tones while giving a scratch to the withers.

A common practice with foals raised on the range is to run them into a chute where they are handled and haltered for the first time. Providing the chute is of the right proportions, confining the young horse this way may involve minimal trauma. Roping the young horse around the neck or legs is rarely practiced today and in most cases is not recommended.

Haltering

Leaving a halter on a young foal is dangerous and sidesteps a very important lesson: haltering. Using the procedure outlined below may seem awkward at first, but it ensures you control of the horse at all times. Become adept at this haltering sequence with an old, patient horse before you attempt it on a young, untrained horse.

Approach the horse from the near (left) side, holding the un-

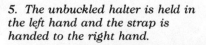

5. The unbuckled halter is held in the left hand and the strap is handed to the right hand.

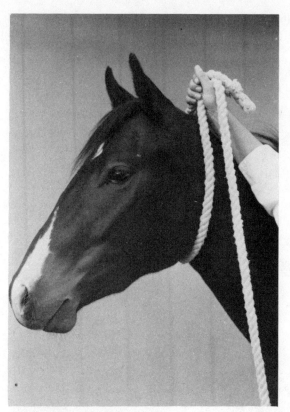

4. Proper haltering procedure begins by encircling the horse's throatlatch with the lead rope held in the right hand.

buckled halter and rope in your left hand. With the right hand, scratch the horse on his withers and then move your right hand across the top of his neck to the right side. Use your left hand to give the end of the lead rope to the right hand, then loop the rope around the horse's throatlatch and hold the loop with your right hand (photo 4). If the horse tries to pull away at this stage, you can pull his head toward you while pressing your right elbow into his neck. Next, pass the halter strap with the holes in it under the horse's neck to your right hand, which is holding the lead rope loop (photo 5). With the left hand, position the noseband of the halter

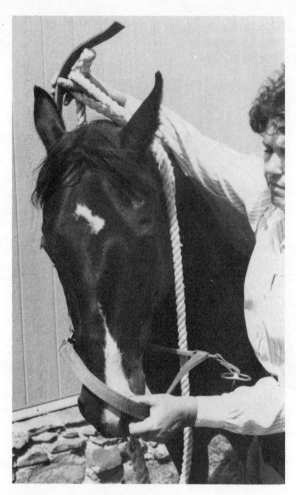

6. *The noseband is raised into position with the left hand.*

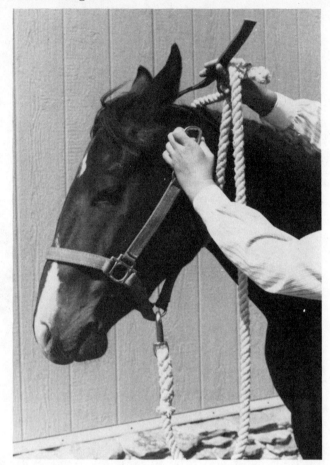

7. *The halter is buckled while control of the neck loop is retained with the right hand.*

on the horse's face (photo 6) and then bring the right hand over behind his ears and use both hands to buckle the halter (photo 7). Be sure the halter is properly fitted (photo 8).

Removing the halter to turn a horse loose follows the same procedure in a somewhat reverse order. Loop the rope around the horse's neck; then remove the halter. Hold the horse momentarily with the loop and then release the loop and gently push him away from you with your right elbow.

Horses can quickly develop a habit of pulling away from their handler in anticipation of their freedom. You must diligently follow a routine until you have established good haltering and unhaltering manners in your horse.

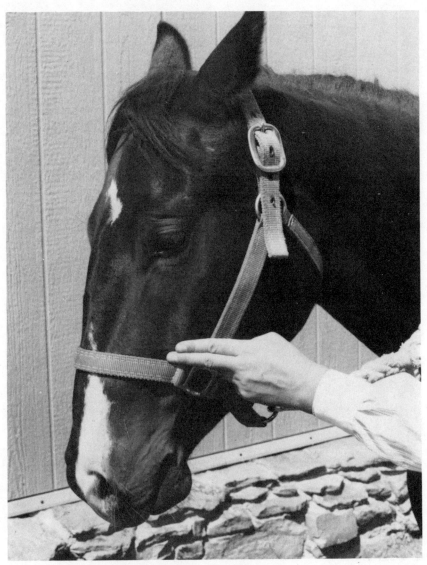

8. *The noseband of the halter should lie approximately two fingers below the prominent facial bone.*

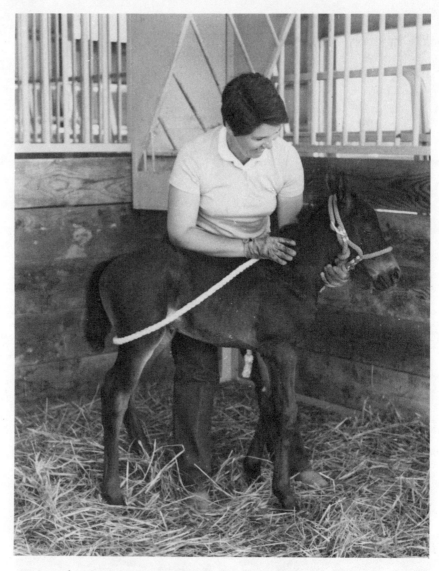

*9. A ten-foot lead rope used as a combination lead
and rump rope for the week-old foal.*

IN-HAND LESSONS I

Equipment:
Whip: 4 to 5 feet long
Rump Rope: 10 to 15-foot 5/8- or ¾-inch cotton rope (photo 9)
Inner Tube: From motorcycle or small car tire
Soft Grooming Brush
Stock Trailer

Once the young foal is caught and haltered, you must begin the basic lessons of in-hand work. "Walk," "whoa," "trot," and "turn" should be sufficient until the foal is several months old.

To encourage the foal to move alongside you, you must convince him to move forward. *Never* pull on the halter to make a young foal move forward. Rather, encourage from behind, with either a light tap of a whip on the rump or a light tug on a rope looped around the rump (photo 10). Regardless which method you use, you should strive to stay in proper position at the foal's shoulder during the lesson. When the foal is moving ahead calmly at your side,

10. *The rump rope offers encouragement from behind for the foal to move forward.*

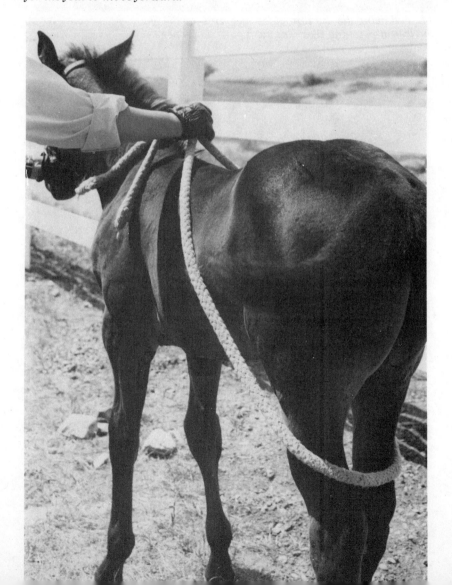

11. *Following the dam provides incentive for the foal to go forward. Note the lesson is taking place beside a fence for control.*

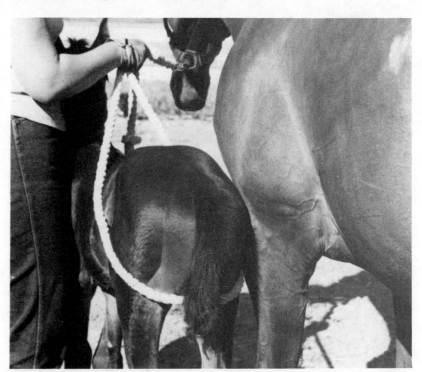

12. *The mare's lead rope can serve a dual purpose as a rump rope for the foal.*

there should be no pressure on the rump rope or inadvertent tapping from the whip. Although it is customary to regularly handle horses from the near (left) side, foals should also be handled from the off (right) side. If you feel any awkwardness, practice with a trained horse until you feel comfortable.

It is helpful to work the foal next to or behind his dam as she is being led by an assistant (photo 11). If the mare is well halter-trained, it is even possible for one trainer to lead both the mare and foal. To do this, use the dam's lead rope as a rump rope for the foal, keeping the foal sandwiched between you and the mare (photo 12).

With his dam nearby, the foal will have incentive to move ahead, and at the same time he begins to move forward your body language and voice commands will say "Walk on!" The foal will begin to associate your movements and command with the proper behavior. Working the foal alongside a fence while he is following the mare will help to teach the foal to track straight (photo 13).

13. *Keeping a position at the foal's shoulder allows the handler to retain maximum control.*

When your assistant starts to stop the mare, you should come to a crisp stop, while applying light pressure to the halter and pushing the foal's head slightly away, toward the fence. These are all signals to slow down or stop. Be sure to use an appropriate voice command such as "Whoa" in conjunction with the physical signals.

An older untrained horse may also need to have a visual barrier, such as the handle of the whip appearing in front of his face, at the same time the other cues are being applied. This may deter his forward advance. Do not hit the horse with the whip, but rather present it visually. A yearling, for example, who has never been handled often attempts to run over the trainer. To avoid injury, you need to use more convincing methods. A chain over the nose is an option more suitable for the weanling; it will be discussed later.

Gently circling the foal behind the dam is the first step in teaching him to turn. When it comes time to teach the foal a 180-degree about-face, however, certain principles should be followed. First, for safety, always turn the foal away from you. When leading the foal from the near side, turn the foal to the right.

From a halt, move your right hand under the foal's neck to the off (right) side while intermittently pressing the butt end of the longe whip or your left fingers on the side of the foal's shoulder. If the foal tends to leap forward, a little backward pressure on the halter will encourage him to settle his weight in his hindquarters for the turn. Later this will help perfect **turns on the hindquarters**.

The young foal will trot a few steps easily and rather automatically. Keeping up with the long walking strides of the dam, the foal will lightly **jog** behind. The best body language from the handler is merely jogging in place next to the foal's shoulder while applying encouragement from the whip or rump rope if necessary.

Tying I

When the foal is several weeks old, he usually can be tied for the first time. Choose a safe place; there is bound to be a reaction. A solid wall with a securely mounted tie-ring is best. If you have to tie a foal to a fence or a hitch rail, be sure the poles or boards are smooth and secure. A horse should never be tied to the horizontal boards of a nailed fence. Boards and rails can become dislodged or break if a frightened animal pulls back, and a terrifying experience can follow if the boards follow the panicked animal. Always tie your horse to a secure post or a well-anchored tie-ring. Horses should be tied at the height of their withers or higher; this makes serious pulling difficult by decreasing the leverage that the horse can obtain with his front legs. Use a quick-release or manger knot to tie a horse to a post (illustration below). The tail end of this knot can be pulled to release a horse in an emergency.

The first few times you tie a foal do not tie him to a solid object. Rather, attach an inner tube to the post or tie-ring where you want to tie the foal so that the lead rope can be attached to the rubber. The elastic effect of the inner tube is much less stressful to a foal's muscles than a solid post would be. If your foal is sullen or resists the pressure on his poll and pulls back, discourage him immediately with a flat smack on the rump or a loud clap from behind. This will usually make a foal jump forward, which relieves the pressure on his poll.

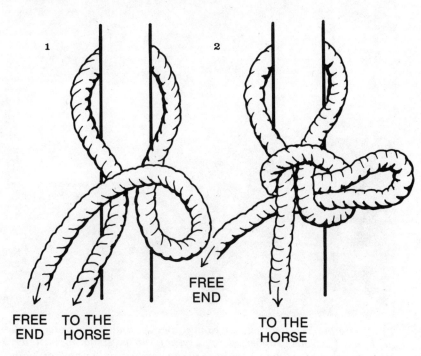

Tying the Quick-Release Knot

Grooming I

At this phase, you should familiarize your foal with gentle handling. For the first few lessons you will not need grooming tools; your hands will suffice. Beginning with the areas of large muscle mass, such as the shoulder and hindquarters, exert moderate pressure with your hands in soothing circular motions. Touching a horse lightly tends to be irritating and encourages movement away from the handler, so you should use steady, firm pressure.

14. *Grooming Tools: Clockwise from upper left and in the order used on the horse: hoof pick; rubber curry (3 types); rubber grooming mitt; terry cloth; mane and tail brush; mane pulling comb; dandy brush or "mud brush"; metal curry comb (used to keep dandy brush bristles clean); body brush; stable rubber.*

15. A wisp is an invigorating grooming tool woven from straw or hay.

Approach the youngster's head carefully, working from the shoulder up the neck. Introduce the head-handling lesson with the foal in hand, not tied, and backed into a safe corner of the stall. Scratching around the foal's ears may cause a violent reaction, so proceed slowly and settle for degrees of acceptance over subsequent sessions. Similarly handle the ribs, flanks, and legs. You may want to have an assistant hold the young horse the first few times you attempt to touch these areas. Remember, it is a natural reflex for the horse to pick up his leg when it is touched, so be ready.

It is advantageous to accustom your foal to having his orifices handled (photo 16). Much veterinary work involves oral, nasal, or rectal entry, so convincing the foal that it is safe to let you touch his mouth, ears, nose, and rectum will result in less trauma later.

The purposes of grooming are as follows.

• To remove dirt, sweat, glandular secretions, dead skin cells, and hair (Sanitation).
• To provide a mental and physical preparation for coming work (Warm-up). The massage increases circulation and relaxes the horse's psyche.

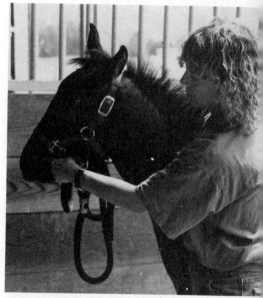

16. Handling the foal's orifices while he is young will result in fewer traumas when veterinary care is administered.

17. *Pressure is exerted by pinching the tendon above the fetlock to teach the foal to pick up his foot.*

- To clean the body and bring natural oils to the surface for a glossy hair coat; to facilitate shedding (Appearance).
- To provide an idle recovering horse with a stimulating and soothing interaction (Rehabilitation).
- To allow the handler to look closely at skin, head, mane, tail, legs, and hooves (Inspection).
- To accustom the horse to being handled and to desensitize ticklish areas (Training).

Hoof Care

Many foals require corrective rasping of their hooves at two months of age or even earlier. If you want your farrier to do his best work and keep coming back to your stable, train your young horses to pick up their feet and hold still for trimming. It is not in the professional code for horseshoers to train your horses for you. It is unfair

18. *A cooperative foal allows the farrier to view the hoof growth and wear patterns.*

19. *This foal has learned to stand on a slack line and is far ahead in his training schedule. For safety, this handler should not be standing directly in front of her horse.*

to expect them to take the time and to risk injury by handling un-ruly youngsters.

Instead of tying the foal for his first hoof-care lessons, have some-one competent hold him alongside a wall or sturdy fence. Having already familiarized the foal with having his legs handled, you will now begin holding his legs for increasing periods of time (photos 17–20).

In the interest of your horse's comfort and your safety, here are some guidelines:

1. Work in close to the horse.

2. Minimize the amount of sideways pull exerted on a horse's leg. Try to lift the leg in the plane it normally moves in: underneath

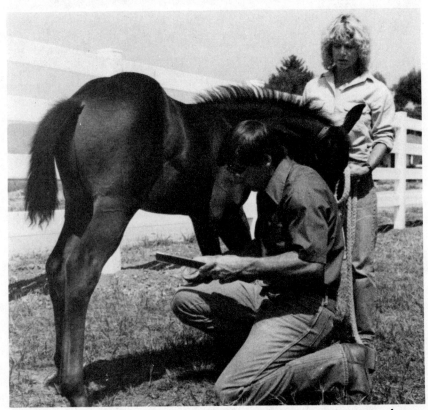

20. The farrier may assume a potentially dangerous position to work on a foal. It is essential that the foal is well-mannered before the farrier's visit so that he can do his best work.

the horse's body. With a tiny foal, this will require crouching and occasional contortions. Be patient. They grow fast!

3. Never let the foal decide when he will put his foot down. Choose a moment when the foal is not struggling to set the hoof decisively on the ground.

4. Push the foal's weight over to the opposite quarter to lighten the leg you are trying to pick up.

5. Don't forcibly pick the hoof up. Rather, squeeze the tendon area or touch the coronary band with the toe of your boot so the foal picks up his own foot. Be ready to catch the hoof in the reflexive action.

6. Once you have grasped the hoof, tip the toe up so the fetlock and pastern are hyperflexed. This tends to block nerve transmissions and reflexes. With very sensitive horses, it helps to hold the hoof rather than the leg.

7. Use body-to-body contact to assure the foal that your grip is not tenuous. Do not encourage leaning. It is not impossible to support one fourth of the weight of a 100-pound foal, but it doesn't take long for him to reach 1200 pounds. Habits remain even though physical proportions change.

8. When working on the hind leg, drape the arm nearest the foal over the hock, and with the other hand, tip the toe of the hoof up. This "hock lock" gives you a leverage advantage in the event the foal tries to pull away.

A knowledgeable farrier usually doesn't mind a curious youngster who briefly inspects him and his tools with polite sniffing. However, he *will* mind ill-mannered nibbling and slobbering when his back is to the horse (which is 90 percent of the time). Practice in advance for the farrier's visit by having a friend monitor your foal's behavior when you are handling his hooves so that he can be taught to stand without nuzzling his handler.

Trailering I

Once the foal has passed his initial in-hand lessons, he is ready to learn to load in a roomy trailer. If you don't have access to a stock trailer or a horse box with a large compartment for both the mare and foal, you should probably postpone such lessons until you do or until the young horse has reached his yearling year. The trailer should be either hitched to a vehicle or the wheels, hitch, and entryway well blocked to prevent the trailer from moving or the foal from slipping under the sill.

Leading the foal into a stock trailer behind a well-mannered mare is the best way to begin the young horse's association with trailers. He can become accustomed to the sound and feel of the hollow floor and the rattle of the dividers. It may take as many as three people to successfully load the young horse the first time: one to lead the mare, one to lead the foal, and one to close the gate. It is good if you can turn both horses loose for a time in a roomy compartment, providing the mare is not nervous. The best introduction to motion for the foal is often hauling him and his dam in a "box stall on wheels." Later on, in more advanced in-hand work, you will teach the horse as a yearling to walk into a single stall of a two-horse trailer.

The Suckling Foal

FIVE

The Weanling

RESTRAINT I

Equipment:

Weanling Halter (photo 21)

Cotton lead shank with chain; the chain is approximately 12 inches long and the lead shank is ¾-inch rope, about 8 feet long. Snap and connecting links should be small enough to pass though the rings in a halter (photo 22).

Twitch: A wooden-handled twitch with chain loop is most effective.

Restraint is the limiting of an action or movement by physical or psychological force. A trainer's voice and hand can be an effective means of restraint, provided the horse has been taught to respect and obey various commands and cues. Often restraint is accomplished by using devices such as ropes, twitches, and chains. Teaching the horse he must submit is not meant to be harmful, but rather to protect the horse from his own natural instincts in the human world. Horses that have gone through well-planned restraint lessons are more likely to remain calm when tangled in ropes or fences, experience less trauma when restrained by the veterinarian for treatment, have better manners for farrier work, and test the limits of their behavior less often. Once a horse knows the meaning of the word "Whoa" with the aid of restraint, he is much safer in routine management situations such as bathing, clipping, vaccinating, deworming, and tacking.

Restraint lessons begin the first time a foal is caught and will span the yearling and two-year-old years. Formal lessons usually are

21. *The young horse's head changes size rapidly. By weaning, the foal is wearing a scaled-down version of an adult-style halter. This halter fits perfectly.*

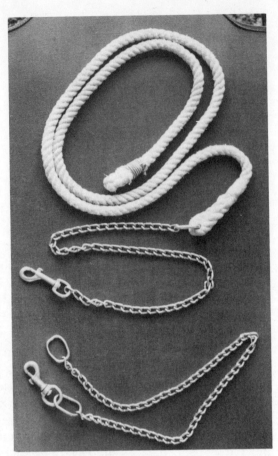

22. *A chain lead shank or a chain that can be snapped to a regular lead rope may be necessary to control the young horse.*

started after a horse has been successfully weaned. To begin, tie the weanling to a solid post (photo 23). The transition is usually smooth if suckling lessons went well with the inner tube. If, however, the weanling persists on pulling when tied, you may have to resort to the use of a **wither rope**. However, first try and solve the problem by checking the previously mentioned guidelines for proper tying. The wither rope is not recommended for a horse younger than a year (see Chapter 6).

Moving Over While Tied

Once the foal has accepted being tied, he must learn to move over while tied. If you approach this maneuver as if it were a **turn on the forehand** (where the hind legs step around the stationary front legs), the lesson will probably go smoothly. If you stand on the off (right) side of a horse that is tied, you will be able to move his hindquarters to the left while his forehand stays stationary by applying pressure to the right rib cage and at the same time turning the horse's head slightly to the right (photo 24). In the interest of connecting this lesson to riding cues, apply pressure to the horse's ribs

24. *To move a horse to the left while he is tied, position his head slightly to the right and press your fingers against the ribs on his right side. Be sure the lead rope allows his head to move without conflicting pressures. This photo shows the last few steps of a turn on the forehand at the rail where the hindquarters have moved to the left.*

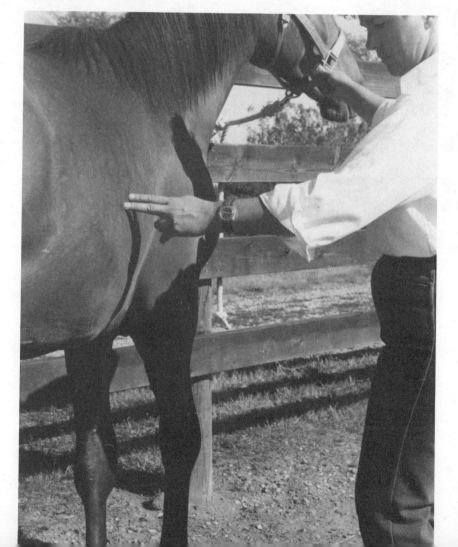

23. *This yearling is tempted to chew the lead rope when tied. A slap on the shoulder coupled with an appropriate voice command should discourage such behavior in a few lessons.*

at the approximate location that a rider's leg will later be positioned. The pressure should be intermittent as should the light tugs on the halter. It is not uncommon for the young horse to swish its tail, look up, or even move into you the first time you apply these aids. Resist the temptation of using brute strength to move your horse over. If necessary, substitute the handle of your hoof pick for your fingers to accent the cue at the ribs. Be sure to work on both sides. Practice this a few times in each direction for several days, and your horse should learn the lesson.

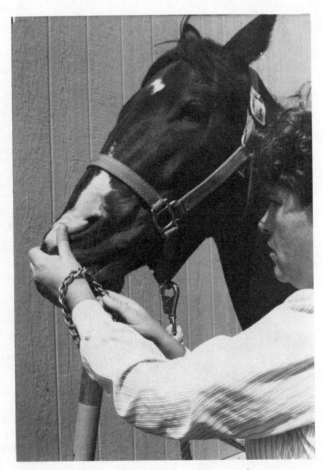

25. *To apply a chain twitch, put the chain loop over your left wrist, take the nose with the left hand, and with the right hand transfer the chain from wrist to nose.*

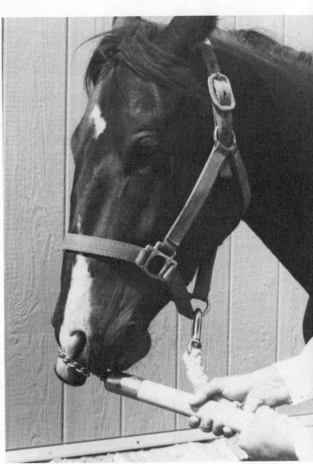

26. *Twist the chain until ample pressure is achieved to control the horse without inflicting unnecessary pain.*

27. After removing the twitch, rub the horse's nose to restore feeling and good will.

Handling for Veterinary Care

A young horse will need frequent veterinary visits for routine vaccinations and deworming and for possible emergencies. Therefore, you should introduce your weanling in advance to the various restraints that may be used.

There are several means of twitching a horse, which is essentially grabbing a portion of skin and exerting pressure. Most commonly, the upper lip of a horse is held by a chain twitch with a wooden handle (photos 25–26). Although twitching was long regarded as a diversionary tactic, it is now thought that application of a twitch accelerates the release of endorphins, the body's natural pain relievers. This creates a state of euphoria in the horse and makes him less likely to react to what might otherwise be disturbing procedures.

After you remove the twitch, be sure to thoroughly massage your horse's nose to restore circulation and to leave him with a more pleasant association for future handling of the area (photo 27).

If no twitch is available, grabbing a handful of shoulder skin and rolling your knuckles inward is a convenient way of restraining a horse (photo 28). It is much better than the ear twitch, which can tend to make the horse head-shy and can even damage the ear.

Chain Positions

A lead shank with a short length of chain on the end is useful in restraining the forward movement of an excited or overanxious animal. It should not be substituted for proper training, but it can give a handler a mechanical advantage over an unruly animal.

The chain can be applied in many ways (photos 29–34). They are listed here in order of increasing severity. Some of the applications are inappropriate for the training of young horses, but are included for the sake of completeness.

Attaching the snap of a chain shank to the halter ring under the jaw of the horse serves no purpose but to force the handler to hold the chain. It is not recommended for any situation requiring restraint.

Using a chain threaded under the horse's jaw encourages the horse to raise his head (photo 29). You might use this chain setup with a sleepy horse who needs to pay attention in halter classes, for example. Otherwise, it is not the most effective means for getting a horse under control.

A chain over the horse's nose is a common and useful means of restraint (photos 30–32). It is essential to use the chain with a well-fitted halter. Thread the snap of the chain first through the throat ring, then the lower near cheek ring, one wrap over the noseband, and out through the lower off cheek ring, and finally attach it to the upper off cheek ring. Using a chain in this fashion prevents it from slipping down to the sensitive cartilage of the horse's nose and keeps halter twisting to a minimum.

The first time you use a chain shank on your horse, he may rear or strike, so be very careful. With a young horse often only a lesson or two is necessary to teach him manners. It is usually unnecessary to use a chain shank on a weanling if he has had proper handling. It

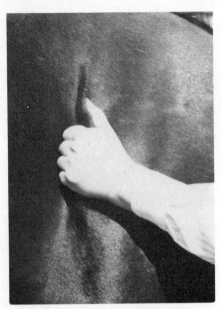

28. *The shoulder twitch is an effective means of subduing a horse.*

29. *A chain shank positioned under the horse's jaw tends to make the horse raise his head when pressure is applied.*

30 and 31. *For overall control, a chain over the nose is preferred.*

32. *A variation of the over-the-nose chain is a chain loop that encircles the horse's nose and snaps to itself under the throat. This may result in less halter-twisting if there is a less-than-perfect halter fit.*

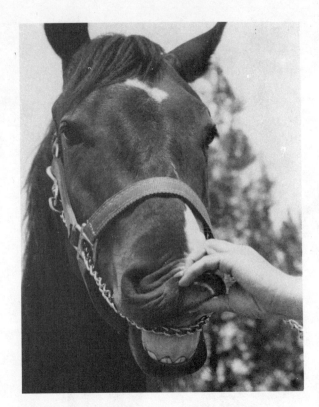

33. *Occasionally an unruly horse is controlled with a "lip chain." Somewhat of a misnomer, it would more correctly be called a "gum chain" as the chain passes over the upper gums and under the upper lip.*

34. *A chain through the mouth is configured much like the over-the-nose style except that the chain passes through the horse's mouth where the bit lies. This is potentially dangerous and should be used with care and experience.*

is best to reserve this device for use on horses one year or older who have not had prior handling or who are difficult to control.

Occasionally a chain is used on the gums, under the upper lip, but this is a very severe method of restraint best left to experienced professionals (photo 33). Running a chain through the mouth as with a bit (photo 34), or over the poll as with a **war bridle** are also very severe methods that should be regarded as last-resort tactics. As with all restraint, indiscriminate use of a chain shank can backfire on an inexperienced handler.

The Weanling

SIX

The Yearling

IN-HAND LESSONS II

The yearling year is a good time to expand your horse's in-hand base to include maneuvers that will be used later when riding and to develop confidence and obedience when encountering obstacles. You will obtain the best results by setting your horse up in proper position and then applying the specific cues for the movement of the desired maneuver. With the yearling, first review all previous in-hand lessons (photos 35–38) before proceeding with the new lessons.

Backing

The first addition to the yearling's in-hand repertoire should be learning to back. A natural way to show him what is desired is to lead him into a narrow passageway that he must back out from to exit. To get your horse to back, turn around and face him, holding the lead rope in your left hand, and use your right hand to apply alternate pressure to the left and right points of his shoulders (photo 39). The back is a two-beat diagonal gait with the left front and the right hind legs moving together and the right front and left hind legs following. Applying alternate pressure to the left and right points of the shoulders of the young horse causes him to start moving backwards in a proper diagonal stride. Walk toward the horse, giving light backward tugs on the noseband of the halter and using a voice command such as "Baaaack" (photo 40). Once your horse makes the connection between these cues you can gradually eliminate all but the one you plan to use permanently.

58

35. *The trainer is in proper position, slightly ahead of the horse's shoulder.*

36. *In a circle to the right, the trainer uses his hand under the horse's throat to move the horse's head to the right. Note the arc of the horse's body, the crossover of his front legs, and the organization of the trainer's body language and equipment.*

37. *Jogging in place is often all that is necessary for you to encourage a horse to trot, but carry a whip for insurance.*

38. *Leading the horse from the off side improves the dexterity of both handler and horse. The handler should be looking in the direction of travel, rather than at the horse.*

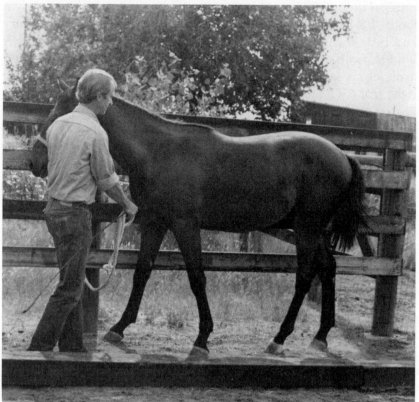

39. Backing in hand might best be introduced with the aid of a fence and a rail.

The Turn on the Hindquarter

Polishing up the turns in hand requires an understanding of the footfall patterns of two maneuvers that will later be used in riding.

When you taught your horse as a foal to circle away from you, he was probably performing a variation of a 180-degree turn on the hindquarter. In this turn the front feet step a half circle around the hindquarters, specifically around a hind **pivot** foot. In Western-style maneuvers, a pivot foot is more firmly anchored to its spot on the ground, changing direction by swiveling. English-style movements require that the stationary foot raises and lowers in proper gait cadence, such as in a walk-around turn on the haunches. In a

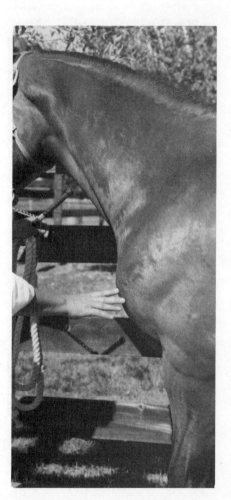

40. Pressing the point of the shoulder while exerting pressure on the halter results in backward movement. The fence helps to keep the horse's movement straight.

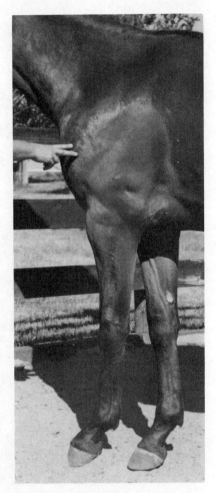

41. *Applying pressure on the outside of the horse's lower shoulder results in lateral movement of the front legs. This horse is completing a turn on the hindquarters to the right. His left front leg has just crossed over his right front leg.*

turn on the hindquarter to the right, for example, the horse's pivot foot is his right hind. The pivot foot should be relatively stationary and bear the majority of the horse's weight in the turn. The left hind leg walks a tiny half circle around the right hind leg. The left front leg crosses over and in front of the right front leg and then the right front leg steps out to the side again (photo 41). This is repeated as the front legs move in a semicircle. To set your horse up for this maneuver, first shift his weight back to his hindquarters with light pressure on the noseband of the halter. Then shift the weight of his front end over to the right side by pushing the lead rope under his neck to the right and at the same time pressing the point of his left shoulder.

To perform the turn to the left you must stand on the off side of the horse, which is usually more awkward for you than for him. The footfall patterns and aids are reversed.

The Turn on the Forehand

When you taught your horse to move over while tied, you were teaching him a rudimentary form of the turn on the forehand. In this maneuver, the horse's hind legs step a half circle around his stationary forehand. If your horse's hindquarters are moving to the right, away from you as you stand on the near side, the horse should be rotating around his left front leg (photo 42).

In order to weight the stationary foot, turn your horse's head and neck slightly toward that foot. This lightens up the opposite forefoot and allows it to step in a small circle around the weighted foot. In order to activate the hindquarters in their larger semicircle to the right, apply pressure at the ribs at the point where a rider's leg will later be positioned.

The aids for a sidepass are a blending of the aids for a turn on the forehand and a turn on the hindquarter (photos 43–44). The horse's head is held straight while pressure is applied at appropriate points at the shoulder and rib to trigger sideways movement.

Halting on the Long Line

Whether for show, photography, or just good manners, all young horses should be taught to stand still on the end of a ten-foot lead rope (photo 45). Although this lesson is usually best accomplished after the hobbling lessons in the fall of the yearling year, the concept can be introduced earlier.

42. *Pressure at the ribs results in lateral movement of the hind legs. This horse is getting ready to step to the right with his left hind leg in a turn on the forehand.*

43. *A side-pass can be introduced by keeping the horse's body straight, exerting slight pressure on the halter toward the desired direction of movement, and applying finger pressure at the ribs. A pole helps the horse understand not to move forward.*

44. As this horse side-passes to the right, he crosses his left front leg in front of his right front leg, then will cross his left hind leg in front of the right hind leg.

45. "Whoa" on the ten-foot lead line.

It is essential that you make a strong connection in your horse's mind with halting and the command "Whoa." Then, even when you leave your usual position at your horse's shoulder, he will be reassured that he is to stand still. If he tries to follow, take him back to the original spot, tug on the noseband of the halter, and say "Whoa." Soon, just stepping toward him assertively while using the voice command should inhibit his wandering. At first, it is adequate to ask your young horse to stand for only five or ten seconds. Gradually build up his patience and attention span.

Obstacles
Taking your yearling for ten-minute walks around your farm or ranch will begin to build his confidence in working with you. Never

ask a youngster to negotiate an obstacle that is unsafe or unfair. Gradually build your horse's willingness to go forward. Your horse will soon trust you and follow you wherever you ask him to go. It is useful for your horse to become familiar with mud puddles, ditches, cement slabs, manholes, culverts, farm machinery, road signs, and unusual animals.

On your excursions carry a long whip in your left hand so you can encourage **impulsion** from behind. It is important to remember that you should always be prepared to go through the obstacle with the horse. If you plan to work on crossing water, wear rubber boots so you can show your horse there is no reason to detour a water obstacle.

If you anticipate problems with a particular object, you may need to use a chain shank along with the whip. Use of the whip to keep the young horse up at your shoulder and the chain to prevent him from rearing or lunging forward teaches him that there is one spot that is safe—next to you in proper position. This same concept will come into play when you ride the horse. You will drive him up to the bridle with your legs and regulate his forward movement with your hands. If you make him understand the relationship between the driving and regulating forces early in life, you will have a much easier time later. He needs to respect but not fear your aids.

Allow ample time for young horses to inspect unfamiliar objects (photo 46). Before actually asking your horse to negotiate a particularly unusual ditch, for example, it is acceptable to allow the youngster to sniff and look, but do not permit even one single step backward. The experienced trainer can tell when a horse is stalling for time and when it is genuinely curious or concerned. Honest inspection is characterized by attentive ears, intense looking, and a reaching forward with the entire body. Often the distinction is not so clear, and the novice may be faced with a horse that balks or refuses to go forward. The best advice is to avoid a confrontation that you are not sure you can win. Often it is helpful to leave the obstacle and review the walk, trot, halt, back, and turn somewhere nearby and then return to the obstacle after the horse has been "tuned up." There are situations where even professionals solicit help from other trainers. Sometimes merely the presence of two people convinces the horse that he must comply.

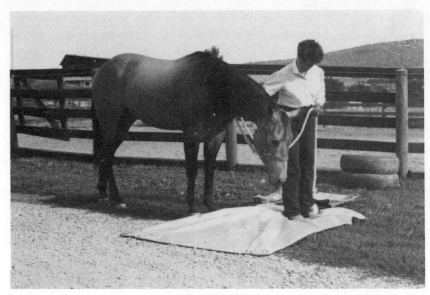

46. *Allow the horse to inspect the obstacle.*

47. *When the plastic moves with the first step, the horse can become apprehensive.*

48. Be sure to insist that the horse's hind legs track straight behind his front legs.

The young horse should be made to walk over rocks, through muddy spots with solid bases, through deep sand, over small fallen trees or branches, and over ground poles and plastic (photos 47–50). All of this will train him for your future requests and will help to develop his dexterity, balance, and confidence.

49. Allow the horse to negotiate ground poles on a slack line so he can look where he is going.

*50. Leading the horse through
puddles will help when it comes
time to ride him across a creek.*

Teaching a horse thorough in-hand lessons will make him a pleasure to handle when in an awkward position such as going through a gate. An untrained horse will make passing through a gate dangerous or next to impossible as he swerves, swings, balks, or backs up at the most inopportune time. Working a gate from the ground requires that the horse knows the previous lessons of the walk, halt, back, and turn on the forehand. You can use a gate to tune up a young horse because the gate is a visual cue that he can easily relate to, especially while backing. Separating going through a gate into its components and training the horse to negotiate them with carefully placed steps will help immensely when it comes time for you to open the first gate from horseback. For example, when opening a gate that swings toward you, walk the horse directly to the latch and halt. Stand for a few seconds. Unlatch the gate and begin opening it toward the horse while using the voice command for back. After the gate has opened about 45 degrees, pause for several seconds. Then ask the horse to perform a 180-degree turn on the forehand to pass through the opening. Pause; back; pause; latch the gate.

Trailering II

Loading a horse in a trailer is a continuation of the "walk on" lesson. While the yearling is in an advanced stage of his in-hand training, you should set aside some time to give him a series of trailer-loading lessons. Customarily, the horse's tail and legs are wrapped for protection (photos 51–52). Although the horse may

51. Leg wraps for trailering should protect the coronary bands and bulbs of the heels.

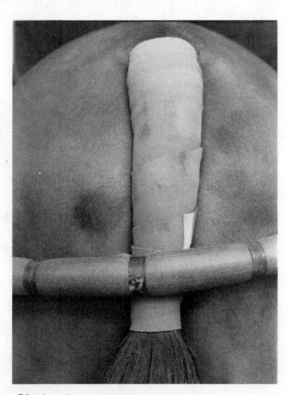

52. A tail wrap will keep the butt chain of the trailer from ruining the tail. This butt chain has been wrapped with foam pipe insulation.

have been in a stock trailer with his dam, there is quite a difference in sending him into a narrow two-horse trailer by himself. At first, you may choose to walk alongside him into the adjacent stall. Load him in the right side of the trailer and walk into the left side yourself. Leading directly in front of the horse into the same side "to show him it's safe" can be dangerous. He may lunge forward and trample you or may attempt to follow you out the escape door.

After being loaded once or twice with you leading alongside, the yearling should enter the trailer by himself with you standing at the back door giving the command, "Walk on" (photos 53–55). Horses should never be coaxed into a trailer by bribing them with feed, but an obedient horse can be rewarded after he has loaded. Having someone stationed at the manger to speak reassuringly to the horse

53. To send the horse into a stall of a two-horse trailer, the trainer assumes proper position.

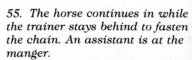

54. *Horse and trainer approach the trailer. The lead has been draped over the horse's withers. The trainer says, "Walk on."*

55. *The horse continues in while the trainer stays behind to fasten the chain. An assistant is at the manger.*

will allow you to stand at the rear of the trailer to secure the doors. Never fasten the trailer tie (usually a twelve to eighteen-inch rope with a panic snap located in the manger of the trailer) until the rear door and/or the butt chain have been secured. Remove the lead rope for traveling.

Things can go wrong. The horse may back out immediately, or attempt to turn around and get stuck. He may rear and put his front legs in the manger. Trailer loading can hold its share of surprises for the novice horseperson. If you are at all hesitant, seek professional help rather than jeopardizing your safety or your horse's.

Often, getting the young horse to back out of the trailer is much more difficult than getting him to enter. In most trailers, there is no way to get next to the youngster to cue him. To get him to unload, first attach the lead rope and unsnap the trailer tie. Then signal your assistant to open the rear doors and unhook the butt chain or bar. Unloading will be easier if you have taught your horse to back up in hand and "weaned" him from all cues except the voice command. Saying "back" will often provide enough of a clue that he will begin shifting his weight rearward. The first step off is a tough one. Many young horses are frightened and jump back into the trailer. If the footing is slippery the problem will be compounded. You can prepare your horse for this and give him confidence by leading him over ledges or bridges. If you are loading without a ramp, be sure your horse's legs will not slip under the trailer sill as he backs out. Never pull the tail to get a horse to unload. Nor should you stand directly behind a trailered horse whether or not the butt chain is fastened.

There are many methods and theories for dealing with problem loaders. Unfortunately, the addition of devices or force at trailer-loading time can be disastrous if the horse has not been made to mind during other ground maneuvers. Therefore, before using a come-along or a butt rope, or resorting to violence, work on your horse's obedience to basic in-hand work. Then tackle the trailer and you will probably be pleasantly surprised.

When it comes time to start the engine and take the yearling for his first ride, it is good to have him ride with a well-traveled companion. With the manger full of fresh hay and a quiet and content old gelding or patient mare alongside, the young horse will relax and enjoy the association with the trailer.

RESTRAINT II

Equipment:

Two 25 to 30-foot-long cotton ropes which are about ¾ inches in diameter. One should have a snap spliced into one end.

Foot strap: Either a burlap loop, a leather pastern strap, or a pony cinch (photos 56–57).

Hobbles: Either a leather figure-eight type or burlap (photo 58).

Front leg strap: Figure-eight hobbles will work here also (see illustration on page 74).

57. *Leather pastern strap.*

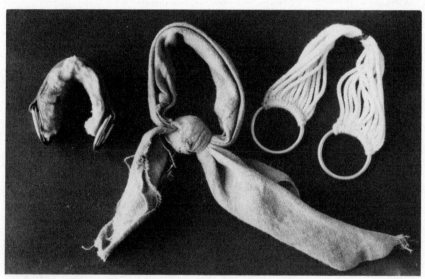

56. *Three choices for hind-leg foot straps: leather with sheepskin lining, burlap sack, and pony cinch.*

58. *Sheepskin-lined figure-eight hobbles that can also serve as a front leg strap.*

Training begins to intensify for the yearling. He will be asked to learn a variety of things quickly. Between twelve and eighteen months of age, depending on his physical development and the weather, your horse should have at least three formal restraint sessions. These are designed to teach the horse to stand still when commanded, which will be useful for later handling. It is of utmost importance that you follow the safest practices possible when restraining horses.

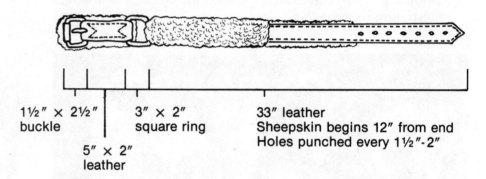

1½″ × 2½″
buckle

5″ × 2″
leather

3″ × 2″
square ring

33″ leather
Sheepskin begins 12″ from end
Holes punched every 1½″-2″

Construction Design for the Front Leg Strap and/or Figure-Eight Hobbles

Facilities

Many of the lessons for the yearling (and the two-year-old) are best performed in a small enclosuré (photos 59–60). For restraint, longeing, driving, and first rides, round pens are superior to square or rectangular pens because they have no corners for the young horse to duck into should he want to evade you . The optimum size is 66 feet in diameter, which is the equivalent of a 20-meter circle. Your horse will be traveling on a 33-foot longe line. A pen this size would also be suitable for restraint purposes.

The round pen should have solid walls or a board fence high enough to discourage a horse from attempting to jump. For most breeds a six-foot height is adequate. A pen with solid walls has the advantage of helping the horse keep his attention focused on you. However, although pens with solid walls are safer than fence-type pens in terms of horse leg injuries, they can present quite a danger if you get pinned against a wall or need to exit the pen in a hurry.

59. *A 65-foot-diameter round pen provides an ideal working area for many of the yearling's and two-year-old's lessons.*

A four- or five-board fence-type pen, on the other hand, allows the young horse to see his surrounding environment. Although the horse can be more easily distracted in an open-style pen, the training that takes place will be more valuable when the horse's lessons are transferred to an arena or open area. The fence-type pen requires eight- or ten-inch boards that are at least two inches thick and a maximum length of about eight feet. Boards spanning a greater distance than eight feet won't provide a secure enough barrier if your horse falls against the wall. Set eight-inch-diameter posts three and one-half feet in the ground and at a five to ten-degree angle so that the walls of the pen tip outward enough to accommodate a rider's legs.

The footing of a round pen should be well drained and furnish adequate cushion. Four to six inches of sand should provide the necessary cover for most activities. For a footing that will be less abrasive on both horse and rider in the event of a fall, work the sand in with the native soil. This may require the same amount of sand but will often give you better footing. Use railroad ties between the bases of the posts to hold the sand in the round pen.

60. *The walls of the pen are slanted outward; boards nailed on the inside and railroad ties are used to hold sand in the pen.*

Protective Measures

Although it is rare for a horse to get hurt when restrained, there are some precautionary measures that should be followed. You should equip your horse with protective schooling boots or wrap his pasterns and knees with bandages to prevent him from getting sand abrasions or rope burns. You should always wear gloves when handling ropes. Be sure that your hair is worn in such a way that it does not interfere with your vision, and if you wear eyeglasses, make certain they are secure. When working with horses you should always wear boots to protect your feet from an errant hoof.

Scotch Hobble

The first time a yearling (or other horse) is **Scotch hobbled** two experienced people should do it. One holds the long head rope and maintains control of the horse while the other handler ties up the hind leg (photo 61). In the event that the horse falls down, it the responsibility of the person handling the head rope to protect the horse's head by exerting upward pressure on the rope as the horse is falling so that the head rolls softly to the ground. This lesson should be taught in a round pen or other enclosed area.

Tying up one hind leg usually convinces a horse that it is possible to stand on three legs and that there is no benefit in fighting. The leg should be tied high enough that the horse's reflexes don't trick him into thinking the leg is almost on the ground. Letting the leg hover just above the ground creates a physical frustration that can lead to a pulled muscle or stringhalt. Tie the leg high. The leg should remain tied until the horse stands for a minute or so without fighting. The negative reinforcement is the removal of the ropes when the horse stands still. The first time, this may take five to ten minutes or more; the second and third lessons often require only two to three minutes per leg.

The procedure is as follows:

1. Attach the snap of one long cotton rope to the horse's halter. This is the head rope and is held by an assistant.

2. Wrap the pastern of the left hind leg with a bandage.

3. Tie a snug loop around the horse's neck with a **bowline** knot using a second long cotton rope (see illustration on facing page). This is the leg rope.

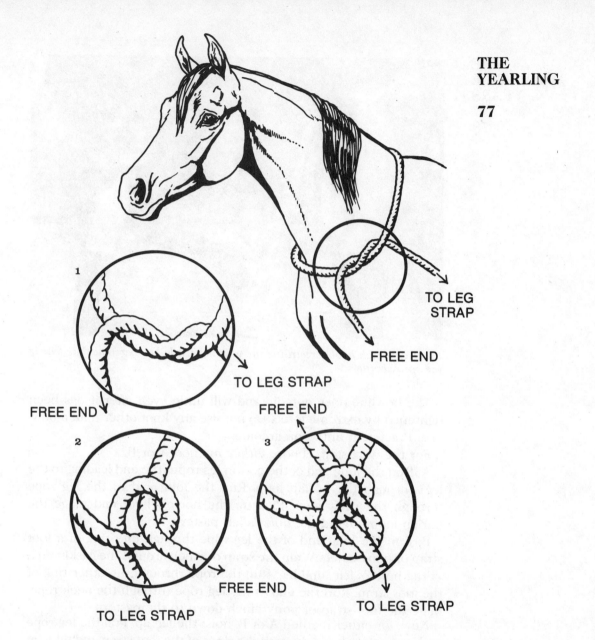

Tying the Bowline
1. *Tie an overhand knot snugly around the horse's neck. With the left hand, pull the free end down and to the right and hand it to the right hand.*
2. *Pass the free end around behind the long end that goes to the leg strap.*
3. *Pass the free end up through the loop from bottom to top.*

61. The Scotch hobble restrains the yearling while he overcomes his fear of the spray bottle.

The bowline does not slip and will untie even after it has been tightened by extreme force. Do not use any knot other than a bowline. Practice it until you are adept.

For the next step, choose *either* method A or B.

A. Run the long end of the cotton leg rope (the end leading to the leg) through the burlap loop. Run the long end of the leg rope through the neck loop. Pick up the horse's hoof and place the burlap loop around the horse's left pastern.

B. Run the long end of the leg rope through one ring of a foot strap or pony cinch. Wrap the strap or cinch around the gaskin area of the horse's left hind leg. Run the rope through the other ring of the foot strap. Run the end of the leg rope through the neck rope. Slide the foot strap or pony cinch down to the pastern.

Now, for either method A or B, hoist the leg up. Pull the leg rope with your right hand through the rings of the foot strap and take up the slack with your left hand where the leg rope comes out at the neck rope. When the fetlock is six to twelve inches below the belly, tie a quick-release knot. Be sure to work quickly but smoothly and keep your fingers out of any loops. Be aware that accidental pulling on the quick-release knot may prematurely release the horse's leg.

The person on the head rope should let the horse stand on a slack rope; however, if the horse starts to fight, she should direct the horse's movement away from the rails of the pen. If the horse tries to put his head down, rather than tug on the head rope, the handler should cast a wave in the rope with an upward flick of her wrist aiming at the underside of the horse's jaw. When the ripple touches the horse, it will make him put his head up. If a horse gets his head down, the neck loop can slide dangerously forward on his neck and cause trouble.

It is not productive to use the command "Whoa" when a horse is testing the limits of restraint. Once you see that he is about to quit fighting, then is the strategic time to use the word. He will later associate it with standing still, even if he is not restrained. Giving praise such as "Good boy" in a pleasant tone will further reassure him that he is doing the right thing.

Problems can occur quickly and unexpectedly when restraining horses, so it is imperative that you have competent, experienced help on hand.

When letting the horse's leg down, be careful not to get **cow-kicked** as the horse begins to feel the restriction removed from his leg. It is a reflex that he will learn to override. Be sure that you decide exactly when he is to put his foot down.

The neck loop can remain on the horse and be used to restrain the other hind leg. Gather up all the rope, rotate it under the horse's neck, and repeat the procedure on the off side. Don't assume that the horse will be good on the off side just because he now is experienced on his near side. Once the horse has accepted this lesson on both hind legs, it is time to move on to the front leg strap. You may cover restraint of all legs in one lesson, or you may have to divide it among several.

Front Leg Strap
The young horse now needs to be convinced that he can stand on two hind legs and one front leg. The front leg strap holds the horse's leg in the flexed position required by the farrier during most of his

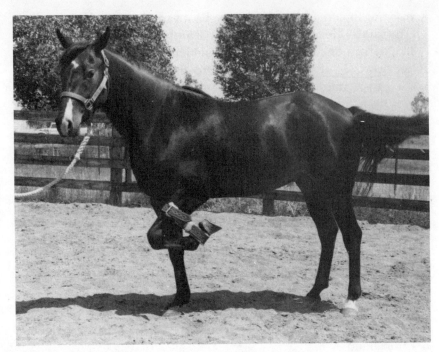

62. *The front leg strap.*

63. *Figure-eight hobbles properly applied on the cannons.*

work (photo 62). The strap keeps the young horse from pulling the leg away, straightening it out, or striking. Note: A strap of the dimensions suggested in the illustration on page 74 and with sheepskin in strategic places can also be used as figure-eight hobbles.

Occasionally a horse will go down on the knee that is restrained and pivot the rest of his body around that leg. Putting wraps over the knees will prevent abrasions. Once the horse has accepted this restraint on both sides, it is time to move on to the most useful restraint: hobbling.

Hobbles

When a horse is hobbled, his front legs are restrained closely together (photo 63). The type of hobbles used to train a horse and the ones used to allow him to graze are two very different pieces of equipment. The latter type characteristically has a length of chain to allow the horse to "hopple" around. Training hobbles, on the other hand, greatly limit movement by keeping the horse's hooves so close they are almost touching. A horse who has not learned to respect restraint through previously mentioned lessons will fight the hobbles and can actually learn to rear, hop, and even run. That is why it is important to introduce the hobbles only after the horse has accepted restraint through Scotch hobbling and use of the front leg strap.

Hobbles should be used around the cannons of the front legs as they are safer there than on the pasterns. Never use hobbles on the hind legs. The strap is "figure-eighted" around the horse's off cannon, then the near cannon, and then buckled snugly on the near side. Leather figure-eight hobbles with a sheepskin lining (as in photo 63) are best for training; however, once your horse knows how to be hobbled you can use burlap hobbles for such tasks such as bathing.

Burlap hobbles are cheap and handy, but may be difficult to untie if the horse has struggled. To make burlap hobbles, remove the seam of a gunny sack, then fold the material into a triangle. Roll the point toward the fold in layers much as you would a bandanna to tie around your neck. Wrap the hobbles around the off cannon, make two tight twists between the horse's legs, and then tie a square knot on the outside of the near cannon. When using burlap hobbles, always carry a sharp knife so you can free your horse easily in an emergency.

Hold your hobbled horse with a long head rope; *never* turn him loose with hobbles. Your objective is to convince him that he cannot move. You should plan to hobble the horse in a formal lesson at least three times in the round pen. While he is hobbled, emphasize that he should stand still by walking around him holding the long head rope but being careful not to accidentally pull his head around with you. Give the rope plenty of slack.

Once you have made a lasting impression on your horse with the hobbling lesson, you can use it to assist you in a number of upcoming lessons, such as bathing, clipping, and saddling.

Sideline

Some horses learn that even though they are hobbled, they can swing their hindquarters, hop, paw, rear, or even canter. If you find

64. The sideline.

your horse needs further restraint to stand still on all fours, there are few options other than sidelining (photo 64). First, hobble your horse's front legs closely and securely. Next, put a foot strap around the pastern of one of his hind legs. Attach the hind leg strap to the middle of the hobbles with a short rope so that when the horse is standing in a comfortable position, the rope is off the ground. Be sure to use a quick-release knot. If the horse kicks with the re-strained hind leg, he will pull his front feet out from under him. If he leaps forward with his hobbled front legs, he will pull the re-strained hind leg out from under him. Be aware that the horse is still capable of kicking with the unrestrained leg. Sidelining is a severe method of restraint and must be administered in a safe place with competent help.

Wither Rope

Occasionally a horse will develop the habit of pulling back when tied. If a yearling has been allowed to break a halter or lead rope and escape from the pressure of the halter on his poll, it is likely he will try to repeat the behavior for quite some time. The best method for dealing with a "puller" is to use a wither rope (photo

65). For this use a 30-foot, ¾-inch cotton restraint rope with an **eye splice** back-braided into one of the ends.

Circle the rope around the heart girth of your horse, passing the free end through the eye splice and then between the horse's front legs. Then pass the free end through the horse's halter from back to front and tie it to a sturdy and safe wall, post, or tree. It is essential that you tie this rope higher than the height of the horse's withers and shorter than a regular halter rope. When the horse pulls, he

65. *The wither rope.*

experiences pressure around his heart girth rather than on his poll, which will usually make him pop forward with a new respect for being tied. This is another means of restraint that should be attempted only with experienced help.

War Bridle
A horse reluctant to move forward might benefit from an in-hand lesson with a war bridle, a "come-along" halter that works by exerting poll pressure to discourage balking or backing up. This halter can be easily fashioned from a lariat (photo 66). Never tie a horse with a war bridle, as he may panic and seriously injure himself.

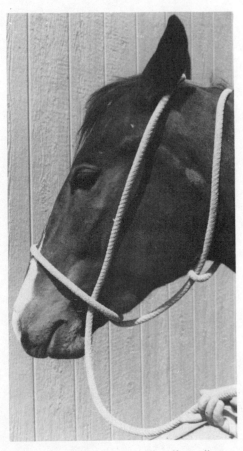

66. *The war bridle or "come-along."*

IN-HAND LESSONS III

Equipment:
   Hobbles, rope, soft jacket or saddle blanket, slicker;
   Electric clippers and extension cord;
   Bucket, sponge, water, aluminum sweat scraper.

Sacking Out
Sacking out is a continuation of the lesson "Whoa." Once your horse has learned restraint, you can begin to build his tolerance for stress. The horse experiences stress when he is forced to change his behavior to adapt to our needs. It is important for the progress of his educaton that a horse learn to handle stress. You should gradually increase your horse's ability to withstand various stresses so that when he is later confronted with them, he will be able to cope.

Self-preservation has taught the horse to be wary of unusual motions, sounds, sights, and smells, and the touch of unfamiliar objects. Setting up a specific group of lessons to help a horse overcome his natural fears will pay off in the long run. When working specifically on building confidence in the young horse, never trigger active **resistance**. In other words, do not stimulate him beyond his ability to cope. If you see your horse get ready to blow up or flee, ease up and gradually work back up to his current tolerance level. Add more stress on another day.

Take the horse into the round pen and hobble him. Show him a soft cloth jacket or a saddle blanket (photo 67). Allow him to smell it, then rub the jacket over his neck, back, and croup. Next, have an assistant hold the horse with a head rope or **ground tie** the horse while you walk around him in a circle softly flapping the jacket (photos 68–69). Gradually increase the intensity of the flapping and decrease the size of the circle you are making around the horse. If he seems ready to explode, stop and let him regain his composure. When he stands quietly for this flapping, increase his tolerance of stress by walking up to him and suddenly flapping the jacket at him. Once he has completely accepted the soft jacket,

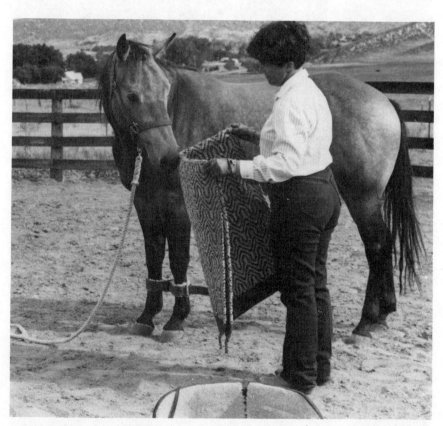

67. *With the horse hobbled, begin the lesson with a soft saddle blanket.*

68 and 69. Be sure to touch the horse with the blanket in his blind spots.

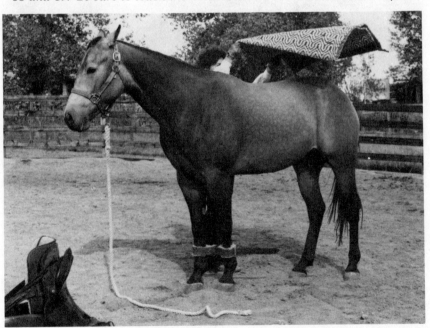

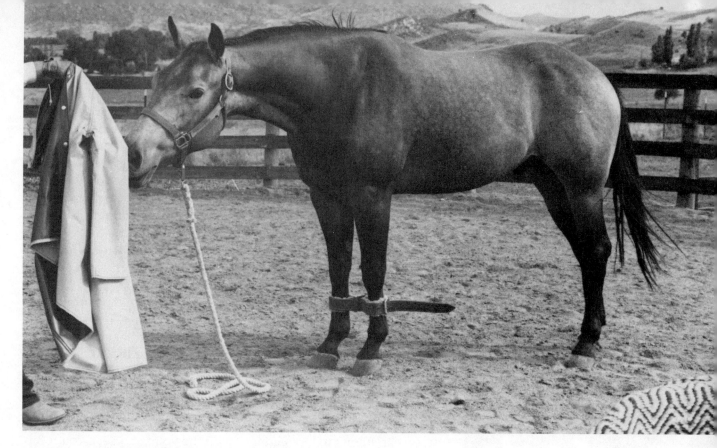

70. Introduce the slicker by letting the horse smell it.

substitute a raincoat or slicker and begin the process again (photo 70).

With the horse still hobbled, swing a rope around him. Drag it on the ground and touch him with it so that he can see it and feel it from all angles. Run it around each of his legs, up between his front legs, and back between his hind legs. Put the rope under the horse's tail being careful not to stand in a dangerous position if he should kick. Tug intermittantly on the rope until your horse learns that if he relaxes, the rope will fall away from his tail.

Use a spray bottle filled with water to prepare your horse for the fly season. Show him that the hissing noise of the bottle and the mist hitting his body are nothing to fear. Other frightening objects you could formally introduce are hats, vehicles, guns, newspapers, blood, and alcohol.

Grooming II

Clipping. If a young horse has accepted being tied, and allows his head and legs to be handled, he will not find clipping very traumatic (photo 71). All that is necessary is to accustom the horse to the sight, sound, smell, and feel of the clippers.

You can choose to introduce your horse to clippers while he is hobbled in the round pen or while an assistant holds him. Whatever your choice, be sure that the electric cord is out of the way, that the clippers are functioning properly, and that the clipper blades are sharp. Begin by letting your horse smell the clippers. Next, rub the clippers on his neck with the motor turned off. Then move to the area of his bridle path and ears (photo 72). Finally, run the clippers down his legs (photos 73 and 74).

Step away so you are standing several yards away from your horse and turn the clippers on and off several times. Then step back to the horse with the clippers off. Lay them on his neck and then turn them on, with the blades facing away from his skin. Let your horse get relaxed with the noise and vibration over this thickly muscled area and then move the clippers to a thin-skinned and bony area. You may need to build up a horse's tolerance to clipping over several sessions.

Be careful not to lose patience with the young horse; if you resort to a twitch while clipping, you may always have to use one. If a horse acts out of honest fear, give him the time and training to over-come the fear. If he acts out of willful disobedience, discipline him.

Horses are clipped primarily to improve their appearance for the show ring or to remove their long coats in winter so they can main-tain condition, dry quickly, and avoid undue stress when being worked strenuously (i.e., hunting) or indoors. However, even the weekend pleasure horse should learn to accept clippers since he too can benefit from some clipping. Clipping a one- to six-inch bridle path (depending on current breed or performance styles) between the forelock and the mane prevents hairs from tangling in a bridle or halter. Removing long fetlock hairs during the especially muddy spring and fall months may deter skin disorders caused from wet and dirty conditions. Many wounds require clipping for thorough cleansing and proper healing. Familiarizing the young horse with clippers at an early age will have a long-term payoff.

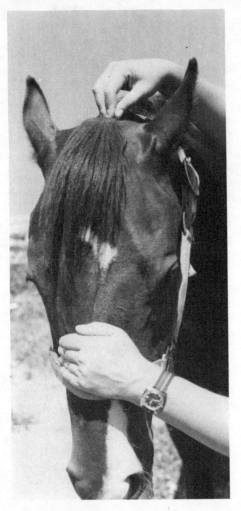

71. *The horse is taught to lower his head with poll pressure.*

73. Clipping the fetlocks is more easily done while holding the horse's leg.

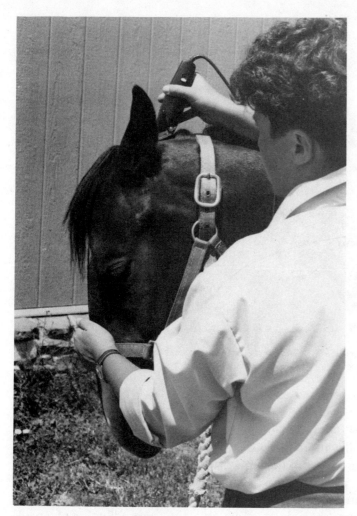

72. Clippers are introduced to this yearling at the poll area.

74. The coronary band can be finished from the ground.

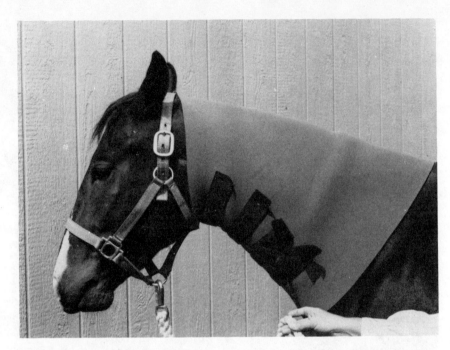

75. *To encourage sweating of a heavy neck, use a neoprene neck wrap during exercise.*

The Neck Sweat. Some young horses begin developing a heavy neck as yearlings. If you are planning to use your horse for performance, you will want to discourage these excessive fat deposits. Using a neoprene neck wrap during work sessions will intensify sweating in the target area, making the neck look sleeker, while muscles in other areas are allowed to continue to build (photo 75). Most horses that have been "sacked out" don't object to the application of a neck sweat. Unfastening the Velcro closures may startle the horse the first few times, however. If you intend your horse to eventually become a breeding or halter horse, you should keep in mind that any alteration in neck size or shape is only a cosmetic masking. The horse still has the genetic potential with which he was born.

Feeding a conservative but adequate diet to young horses, allowing them to ingest forages from ground level, and providing them with the right kinds of exercise will usually discourage heavy necks.

Bathing. Letting a person give him a bath is contrary to a horse's natural sense of self-preservation. Baths can be cold and noisy; they involve unusual equipment and are most notably wet. Asking a horse to stand under a huge rubber snake that is spewing icy water over his back and between his hind legs is certainly unreasonable from his point of view.

It would be ideal if you could schedule your horse's first bath on a hot day when he would possibly appreciate it. Start with a bucket and sponge, rather than a hose, and use body-temperature water so that your horse won't experience a radical temperature change. First, slowly wet his shoulder area with the sponge. Then move on to the back, hindquarters, and then the neck and head. After you have sponged him all over, remove excess water from his body with a contoured aluminum sweat scraper. The dripping water, from the belly especially, can be irritating to the horse. When you are done, tie the horse (or graze him on a lead) in a warm, shady place to dry.

The first bath should be just a quick rinse with water. Using shampoo would require a long rinsing session, which could stretch the lesson beyond the horse's stage of tolerance. In further lessons you can introduce shampoo and the hose. However, even with an experienced horse, avoid using a hose if possible when washing the head. Spraying the face may understandably cause resentment and could lead to ear and eye irritations.

PONYING

Ponying the young horse on the surface he is to be worked on as an adult is a very good way to provide vigorous exercise for the yearling as well as to accomplish other training goals. With an uncastrated yearling colt, however, ponying can be risky, especially if you are forced to use a mare as your **pony horse**. If this is the case, it would probably be best to save this lesson until four or five days after the colt is gelded.

Successful ponying requires an experienced rider and a seasoned pony horse. To tolerate the shenanigans of a yearling requires extreme patience from the pony horse. He must be calm and responsive to the rider or the situation can rapidly become dangerous.

76. *The yearling may be understandably reluctant to travel near the potentially dangerous area of the pony horse.*

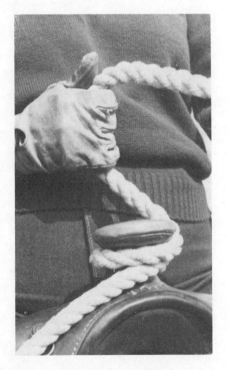

77. *If necessary, dally the lead rope around the horn. Be sure to keep your thumb up and out of the way of the rope.*

Although the yearling may try to bite, rear, kick, or balk, the pony horse should under no circumstances discipline the youngster; that is the rider's responsibility. The pony horse must be assertive without being aggressive. There are situations, however, where the herding instinct of a pony horse is useful: for example, he can help you gain control of the yearling by pushing him in a tight circle.

For a safe ponying lesson, you must either be an experienced horseperson or ask one to help you. There are times when the rider must be appropriately demanding, forgiving, or understanding of the yearling. A balance between discipline and cooperation must be achieved.

In the first lesson, if your young horse is hesitant and apprehensive about traveling so near to an unfamiliar adult horse, you should be firm but reassuring (photo 76). However, if the youngster continues this behavior and starts balking, you must impress upon him that he is to stay near your shoulder just as in working in hand.

This is best accomplished using a Western saddle with a horn so that you can "**dally**" the rope (photo 77). For safety's sake, always wear gloves and remember to keep your thumb up and out of the path of the rope. Keep the yearling's head somewhere in the vicinity of your right knee and the pony horse's shoulder (photo 78). This way you can keep an eye on the yearling, watching for signs of an upcoming nip. If you let your yearling drift behind you and the pony horse, it is very dangerous. In this lagging position, the yearling knows it may get kicked, so may act in panic. For this reason, it is imperative that you keep the yearling in proper position and only pony from a reliable horse.

78. Keeping the yearling's head at the rider's knee allows for maximum control when ponying.

79. *Once the yearling relaxes, the ponying can proceed to work at the trot.*

Pony work is best done at the jog or **long trot** (photo 79). The speed of these gaits is usually similar between horses, and it will make it easier for you to keep the two horses synchronized. The walk and **lope** (or canter) both have a wide variation in speeds between different horses. You could easily get way ahead or behind, causing unnecessary problems.

The first several ponying lessons should take place in the round pen. You will usually have a confrontation with the yearling; he must learn that the pony horse and rider are in charge. Once this lesson is firmly established, it is safe to venture to a large arena and then into wide open spaces. Remember that good footing is crucial for the unshod yearling, so choose your exercise area wisely.

You can gain additional control over the yearling by putting a chain over his nose. This will also encourage him to remain light and very obedient to the pony horse's changes in speed and direction.

Ponying offers a perfect opportunity for you to handle the young horse on the neck and withers from above. You can also move a jacket over the yearling's back at this time as an additional sacking-out lesson.

The Yearling

SEVEN

The Long Yearling

LONGEING

Equipment: 35-foot longe line (photo 80), **Cavesson** (photo 81), Halter or **Bosal** (photo 82);
6-foot longe whip with 6 to 8-foot lash;
Splint boots, and **bell boots** (photo 83);
Circular pen 66 feet in diameter or square pen 66 feet per side;
Gloves for handler, Timepiece.

The long yearling (approximately eighteen months old) should be introduced to very basic longeing. The benefits and uses of longeing are vast and will extend well into the horse's adult life.

80. A 35-foot longe line hand-braided by the author from parachute cord.

96

81. *A longeing cavesson.*

82. *A bosal may be used in place
of a longeing cavesson. The heavy
rawhide noseband gives the
trainer more "whoa power" as the
longe line exerts its pressure from
the rear rather than the front as
with a cavesson.*

Training Benefits:
- Teaches obedience to voice commands and body language.
- Is a progressive step in the horse's education that facilitates the transition from in-hand work to mounted work.
- Gives the horse added confidence by promoting familiarity between horse and trainer, which adds a margin of safety for mounted work.
- Allows supervised time for the horse to become accustomed to carrying an "inert" **snaffle**.
- Introduces principles of **vertical** and **lateral flexion** and gait **extension** and **collection**.
- Corrects bad habits such as moving at an impure gait, head tossing, or avoiding puddles. The repetitive exercise and continuity of a circle help the horse to establish rhythm, to work in certain confines, and to be obedient.

General Benefits:
- Exercise and conditioning: Allows the horse to develop balance, **suppleness**, strength of back and loin, and tendon and ligament durability.
- Valuable for returning a horse to work after illness or injury.
- Good for warmup and cool-down.
- Allows the trainer to view the horse while he is in motion to assess his abilities, lamenesses, or ways of approaching obstacles.

Advanced Training Benefits:
- Can be a beneficial means of giving rider lessons.
- Can be used in introducing **cavalletti** work and jumping.

In spite of longeing's benefits, it can be overused. If you longe your horse routinely before mounting him, it can create a time-consuming dependency. You may, however, need longeing to relax and prepare a hot or well-conditioned horse for more advanced training.

Working a horse in a circle of any size strains his inside legs and may result in lameness. This uneven stress can be minimized by adhering to the following recommendations. On the longe, long yearlings should primarily be walked and trotted to gradually condition their legs. Add cantering only to teach the depart (see page 106).

83. *Splint boots and bell boots.*

Cantering puts as much as 2000 pounds of pressure on the leading foreleg and should be avoided as a means of conditioning until the horse's epiphyses have closed (see page 185).

Longeing a horse too often can also become boring for both trainer and horse. To prevent this from happening, ask your horse for many transitions and work him on varying sizes of circles.

Longeing can create stiffness and bad habits if sessions are improperly designed. You should always be conscious of developing and maintaining contact with the horse through the longe line, keeping the horse round and balanced with your whip position and body language, and regulating the horse's impulsion with a variety of voice commands. If your horse is allowed to circle left with his head, neck, and shoulder pulling to the right, he may carry this habit over to when he is ridden.

Finally, longeing may not be appropriate for all young horses. A roping horse, for example, may have difficulty differentiating a stretched header's rope from a longe line and may begin circling just when his rider wishes him to hold a steer taut.

Because a young horse makes frequent missteps because of his physical inexperience, lack of coordination, and lack of conditioning, it is wise to protect his front legs with boots (photo 83). A stiff pair of splint boots with hard strike plates may prevent a fractured splint bone if the youngster raps his inside cannon with the opposite front hoof. They may also protect the flexor tendons from the blow of a hind toe if he overreaches. Bell boots will protect the bulbs of the front heels from a similar circumstance. They will also minimize trauma to the coronary band if the youngster inadvertently steps on himself.

If a horse has a very solid in-hand base, longeing should pose no great difficulty. Although special longeing equipment is available, you can also teach your horse to longe successfully in a halter. If he is too hard to stop you can add a chain over the noseband of the halter to give yourself more "whoa power."

For the Western horse, you can use a properly fitted and balanced bosal for longeing (photo 84). The bosal, which is actually the heavy rawhide nosepiece of the entire "**jaquima**" or hackamore rig, delivers its pull from the **heel-knot** area. It is suspended from a browband headstall which has had the throatlatch removed and replaced by a knotted rope **fiador**. The hackamore knot is tied

84. The Western horse can learn the same longeing maneuvers and commands with the bosal as the English horse does with a cavesson.

and affixed to the heel knot of the bosal, and the fiador knot is tied and positioned four to six inches above the hackamore knot. The ends of the fiador pass through the headstall at the poll and are secured with a sheet bend knot at the horse's cheek. A bosal is useful for in-hand work, longeing, and riding.

A longeing cavesson is the preferred headpiece for the longeing of young English horses. The longe line's attachment at the front or side of the weighted noseband gives added leverage for control (photo 85). It is not as effective as a bosal at producing a prompt halt, however.

"Bridling" of the yearling with the cavesson or bosal is a lesson in itself. Teaching the horse to lower his head and let you handle it will make bridling with a bit easier. You can also put a snaffle bridle without reins under your yearling's halter, cavesson, or bosal during longeing lessons to let him become familiar with a bit in his mouth.

Select your longeing vocabulary ahead of time; this will help you be consistent in the young horse's first lessons when he needs to know in exact terms what is being asked of him. You should carry over the commands for walk, trot, whoa, and back from your in-hand work. You must add commands for:

- cantering or loping, such as "Can-ter!" said with relatively high pitch and rising inflection;
- extending gaits, such as "Trot on!"
- slowing a gait or calming a frightened horse. Use soothing tones and a falling inflection, such as "Eeeeeeasy";

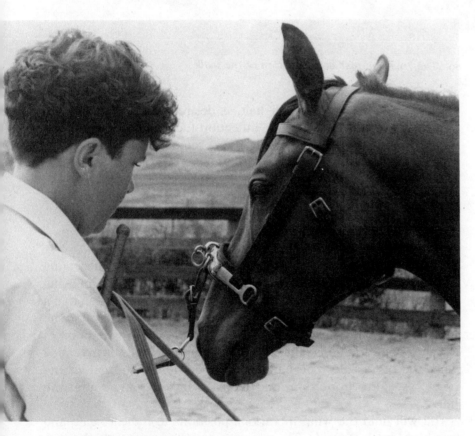

85. *Fitting of the cavesson.*

86. The "piece of pie" configuration at the walk.

- changing direction from a halt, if desired. Using "Turn" with stretched and slightly falling inflection (accompanied by appropriate body language, as in all cases) seems to get the message across. (Cautions against using too many turns on the longe line will be mentioned later);
- letting a horse know he has done something wrong, such as "Uh-uh";
- warning that a command is coming, such as "OKay... (Whoa)" or "Aaaand... (Canter)."

Before the first lesson, you should turn out or pony the young horse to burn off any surplus energy he may have. During longeing lessons, and especially in a round pen, the aerial configuration that a trainer and her horse makes is like a piece of pie rotating around the pie pan (photo 86). The horse is the crust, the trainer the point of the slice of pie, the longe line one side of the slice, and the extended whip the other side. The hand holding the longe line guides the horse, regulates impulsion, and helps to balance and round the horse.

You will hold the whip in various positions to indicate gait, and rate and length of stride. These positions will vary slightly depending on the energy and training level of the horse. Ideally, the horizontal position is used for trot, a 30- to 45-degree elevation from that is used for canter, and a similar drop below the horizontal is used for walk (photos 87–89). For added encouragement, you can send waves through the lash of the whip, roll the whip in circular motions behind the horse, pop the whip, or actually let the lash snap the horse on the top of his croup (this tends to make a horse drop the croup and move on). Do not whip the hind legs even slightly as this can encourage kicking. With a lazy horse, you should not attempt any encouragement with the whip until he is at least twenty feet away from you.

In early longeing lessons, you may have to temporarily vary your position to a little further behind the horse to encourage impulsion and to prevent him from turning to face you. If you allow your position to shift ahead of the horse's midpoint you may inadvertently be telling him to stop or turn. Once your horse has mastered his lesson, however, you may assume the "piece of pie" configuration.

87. *At the walk, the horse tracks quietly on twelve feet of line.*

88. Ask the horse to trot energetically by temporarily raising the whip and saying, "Trot on!"

In the first lessons it may also be necessary for you to walk along in a concentric circle to keep control. Soon you will be able to stand in the center of the round pen and pivot in one spot as the horse works around you. Later on, the concentric-circle method is used when you want to increase your horse's impulsion; it is used with "Trot on," for example, to develop a trot with more reach.

In your first longeing lesson you should start by getting distance between you and your horse. Leave your horse on a slack ten feet of line before giving the first command of "Walk on" (photo 90). (The previously learned "Whoa" on the long line will be useful here.) Walk the horse in each direction, halting him a couple of times, for about five minutes. This will suffice for the first longeing lesson.

Unfortunately, more problems seem to occur at the walk, so you may find it necessary to hold the first several lessons at the trot. This will result in fewer unwanted turns and halts and less confusion.

89. *This energetic yearling needs little encouragement to canter, so the whip is held at a lower level.*

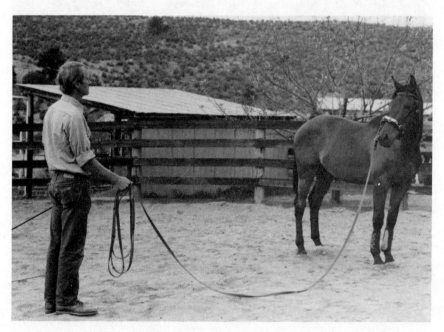

90. *"Whoa" on the longe line should progress to pauses of fifteen seconds or more. This develops patience and obedience.*

During the fall of your horse's yearling year plan one month of three workouts per week. Begin with five to ten minutes of longeing the first week, concentrating on your horse's obedience at being bridled and at the trot, walk, and halt. Begin the work on a ten-foot line and gradually work up to a twenty-foot line, being sure to still maintain control. The second week, increase the length of the lessons to fifteen minutes per session, extend the line to its full thirty to thirty-five feet, and add more trotting. The third week, introduce turning and the canter departure and increase the session length up to twenty minutes. Limit your canter work to two circles at a time, two times in each direction. The fourth week, you can increase your session up to twenty-five to thirty minutes with three canters in each direction (you should still only circle your horse twice at a time). The horse has then learned the basics and can be turned out until he is a two-year-old, at which time you will review and augment these lessons.

91. At first, the yearling may resist the weighted nosepiece.

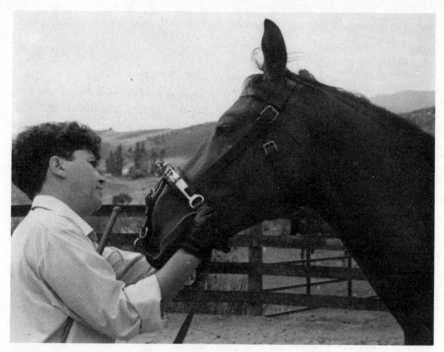

92. Care must be taken to assure that pulling has not caused the cavesson to shift off center.

In this month you are apt to encounter situations you did not expect. Here are some of the common problems and their solutions.

• **Playfulness**

Problem: The horse runs, bucks, and does not pay attention.

Solution: The horse needs to be turned out or exercised before longeing. Never take a young horse fresh from his stall and expect him to pay attention and learn a new lesson.

• **Disobedience**

Problem: The horse cannot be stopped, wraps himself in the longe line, stops and whirls in the opposite direction, or is willful (photo 91).

Solution: Check the headgear to be sure it is properly fitted and gives a firm signal to the horse when pressure is applied (photo 92). Go back and review the in-hand work and insist on obedience. If necessary, review restraint and some sacking-out with ropes.

- **Laziness**

Problem: The horse is sluggish or refuses to move.

Solution: Be sure the horse is healthy and well fed. A horse with parasites, respiratory infection, or inadequate diet may lack energy and initiative. Ensure that the horse's feet are comfortable working on the longeing surface, and have your farrier assess the long yearling's possible need for front shoes during the month of longeing training. If, after assuring that your horse is healthy and comfortable, you still have trouble with laziness, use the whip sharply once on the top of his croup to wake him up. Do not merely threaten your horse by coming close with a wiggling whip or tapping him lightly with it; that will desensitize him to this very important driving aid. It is more humane and effective to use a whip once and with optimum intensity.

- **Pulling**

Problem: The horse pulls against you, dragging you along.

Solution: Use intermittent tugs or jerks on the line. These are more effective than steady pressure to lighten a strong horse.

- **Boredom**

Problem: The horse no longer pays attention to you , his transitions are slow, and cues need to be repeated.

Solution: Assess your voice commands and body language and be sure they are being used with enough intensity. Give a command nicely once and if you are ignored, back up your request with an appropriately forceful aid. Do not use a command over and over again once your horse is doing what you want. It is not necessary to continue to say "Trot, trot" once the horse is trotting. This may dull him to your transition commands. Keep cues sparse and effective.

Change the area you longe in for variety in environment. This will wake up most horses, although it may present a control problem if you longe in an open area.

Introduce a more advanced aspect to longeing, such as gait extension and collection, longeing over a few ground rails or irregular terrain, or longeing with **side reins** or a saddle (see Chapter 8).

- **Cutting corners**

  Problem: The horse does not track a perfect circle but rather makes one portion flat.

  Solution: When your horse cuts in, take a giant step toward him with whip in hand as though you were fencing. You can also add at the same time a command like "Go on!" or "Move out!" Never compensate for your horse's irregular circle by backing up when he travels closer to the center. Instead, make him move out and take contact with the longe line.

- **Shying**

  Problem: The horse veers into the center when he passes something unfamiliar on the rail.

  Solution: Review in-hand and obstacle work.

- **Stiffness or lack of balance**

  Problem: The horse carries himself stiffly or travels heavy on the forehand.

  Solution: Postpone longeing until you can introduce side reins or ground-driving.

EIGHT

The Two-Year-Old

INTRODUCING THE HORSE TO TACK

Equipment:
Snaffle bridle with brow band.
Saddle or **surcingle** (photo 93).
Side reins (photo 94).

The Bridle
Bridling.   There are no new lessons involved in bridling the young horse for the first time (photo 95). He is used to having his ears and head handled, he knows to lower his head with poll pressure, and he has learned to open his mouth for deworming. However, it is critical that you select and adjust the bit very carefully.

Anatomy and the Bit.   The movement of the snaffle bit in a horse's mouth can be affected by the stage of development and the condition of his teeth (see Chapter 11, pages 151 through 157). It is also affected by the texture and sensitivity of the **bars**. Because the fineness of the bone and the thickness of the skin covering of the lower jaw vary among breeds (and between individuals within a breed), there is a wide range of sensitivity of the bars among horses. While a horse's exterior facial structure and fleshiness may indicate what kind of bars he has, the only way to truly ascertain this is to inspect his mouth.

The horse's tongue is a large, thick muscle—one of the strongest in the body. The hyoid apparatus, a five-bone framework, anchors the tongue in the lower jaw. The epithelial cells that cover the horse's tongue are thinner and softer than, for example, a cow's, a pig's, or a dog's. This velvety coating adds to the horse's sensitivity and response to the bit. As with the bars, the size, shape, and covering of the horse's tongue can vary among breeds and between individuals within a breed.

110

The hard palate, or roof of the horse's mouth, is a mildly concave structure formed by eighteen to twenty curved ridges pointing forward. Some horses have a shallower or deeper palate than normal. It is thought that the shallower the roof, the more sensitive the horse will be to bit pressure. This is true with bits designed to act on the roof of the horse's mouth, such as leverage bits with ports. With the snaffle, if the bit is too wide for the horse's mouth,

93. *A surcingle can be used to introduce the horse to the pressure of a girth or cinch.*

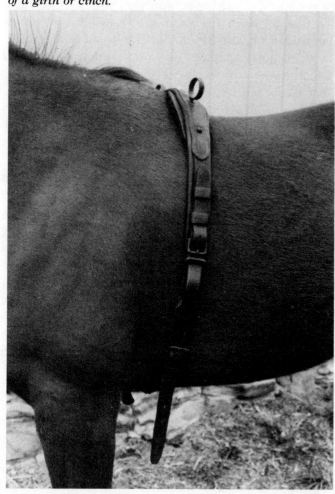

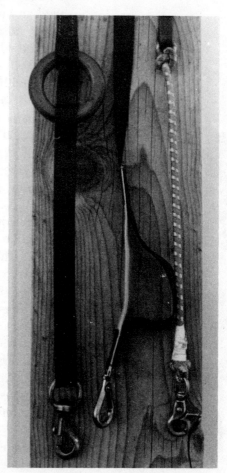

94. *Side-reins from left and in order of increasing flexibility: leather reins with rubber donuts, nylon reins with elastic inserts, and homemade bunji reins.*

its hinging action can cause it to actually peak into the hard palate (especially if the horse's mouth is held closed with a noseband).

The corners of the horse's lips are perhaps the first portion of the horse's mouth that comes to mind when envisioning snaffle action. Besides aiding the rider in turning left and right, the corners of the horse's mouth are an important link in elevation and collection. In **dressage**, for example, a slight upward pressure on the corners of the mouth, along with other aids, encourages the horse to carry its head and neck higher than in either the hunter or Western frame.

The nasal bone and cartilage and the chin groove are often affected when a noseband is used in conjunction with a snaffle. The horse who attempts to open his mouth to avoid bit action is thwarted by the pressure of the noseband. The broad-nosed, thick-skinned, cold-blooded horse may not be as sensitive to a **dropped noseband** as a finer-boned, thin-skinned type.

The poll is not usually affected by the snaffle bridle, with the exception of the gag snaffle. The reins and headstall of the gag are virtually one continuous piece. When the reins are pulled, the headstall shortens. Pressure is exerted on both the poll and the corners of the lips.

Selecting a Snaffle. The most suitable bit for a young horse is the snaffle. The snaffle bit utilizes direct pressure only. There are no **shanks**, therefore no leverage is involved. **Curb** bits, which are not suitable for use with the young horse, have additional control features: the leverage factor related to the length and curvature of the shanks and the shape and dimensions of the port. The mouthpiece of a snaffle can be jointed or solid. The misconception that any bit with a jointed mouthpiece is a snaffle has given rise to the misnomers "long-shanked snaffle," "Tom Thumb snaffle," and "cowboy snaffle," all of which are really jointed curbs.

To assess the effect of a snaffle on a horse's mouth, you should first understand the factors that affect bit severity (photos 96–98). They are:

- the sensitivity of the trainer's hands;
- the thickness of the mouthpiece;
- the weight of the mouthpiece;
- the texture of the mouthpiece;
- the shape or design of the mouthpiece;

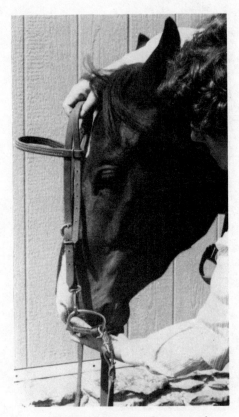

95. *The horse has been taught to lower his head for clipping and open his mouth for deworming. Bridling comes easily.*

96. *The thin mouthpiece of the bradoon creates a more severe signal than the thicker hollow-mouth D-ring snaffle. Both are made of stainless steel.*

97. *The double-twisted-wire snaffle is more severe than the smooth-mouth flat-ring hunt snaffle. The rubber bit guards prevent pinching. Both bits are made of the nickel alloy Never-Rust.*

98. *Commonly used Western snaffles: copper and stainless-steel roller D-ring snaffle, stainless-steel D-ring snaffle, and Don Dodge snaffle with copper-inlaid mouthpiece.*

- the type of metal of the mouthpiece;
- the width of the bit;
- the adjustment of the bridle (and noseband if used);
- the types of rings or spoons.

A trainer's hands have the greatest effect on the horse's mouth, regardless of the bit being used. They have the capacity to turn the mildest bit into an instrument of abuse or the most severe bit into a delicate tool of communication. Above all, good horsemanship is the key to your horse's acceptance of the bridle.

When choosing a snaffle, you should generally select thicker mouthpieces for young or very sensitive horses. The thinner the mouthpiece, the smaller the surface area that receives pressure from your rein aid. The same intensity of pressure is concentrated over a smaller area, therefore the sensation is more intense. To illustrate, press the handle of a butter knife on your index finger. Then press the knife's blade edge on your finger. Which is a sharper signal? Extremely thick mouthpieces should be avoided because there often isn't room for all of that hardware in the horse's mouth.

Commonly, thick-mouthpiece snaffles weigh more because of the additional material needed to make them. This can be an advantage in that weight stabilizes the bit in a horse's mouth. Extreme weight, however, can tire the horse as he attempts to balance the bit. Adding excessive weight to the horse's already heavy head can contribute to heaviness on the forehand. Some large-mouthpiece bits are hollow to provide mild action without excessive weight.

If a bit is extremely thin and light, it may not provide the necessary substance the horse requires to learn to hold the bit in his mouth and take contact with it. Such a bit may make a horse feel less secure and result in an inconsistent frame or top line.

Since the snaffle comes in contact primarily with the bars, the tongue, and the corners of the lips, the texture of the bit's surface will affect its severity. A smooth-mouthed bit makes regular contact with the skin surfaces and underlying nerves. A twisted-wire bit's rough surfaces make interrupted and changing contact, which can jangle nerves and rub tissues raw if the bit is used indiscriminately.

The shape and design of the mouthpiece can instantly affect a horse's response. Due to the variation in horses' mouth structures, certain horses need more room for their tongues. Some with a shallow palate need a bit that will not peak in their mouth. Some horses need pacifiers and others need moisturizers. Rollers, keys, straight bars, Dr. Bristols, and mullen mouths are all designed with the same goal in mind: keeping the horse's tongue happy and responsive. A horse who actively works the bit in his mouth with his tongue while keeping his mouth closed tends to have a moist, soft mouth.

Nerve impulses, which are tiny electrical transmissions, are more efficient when sent through moist tissues. Therefore, a moist mouth is potentially a more responsive mouth.

The salivary reflex is triggered by the presence of food in the horse's mouth. When a horse is bridled, this reflex may be activated by his mouthing of the bit, the construction of the bit, and possibly the vertical position of his head. The metal from which the bit is made can also enhance sensitivity. Metals vary in their chemical and physical properties and their subsequent effect on salivary glands, with copper mouthpieces or mouthpieces inlaid with copper traditionally at the head of the list of saliva-producers. Never-Rust, a yellowish, soft nickel alloy that is very popular in hunter bits, also enhances salivation. Stainless steel and cold-rolled steel are other metals that produce moist mouths. Aluminum, on the other hand, does not. It is a dry, light metal, not often used in snaffles.

The width of the bit can affect its comfort and, inadvertently, its severity. A bit that is too wide for a horse may hang low and bang his canines or incisors, or may encourage the horse to put his tongue over it. An overly wide bit may also peak upwards and scrape the roof of the horse's mouth. A bit that is too narrow can pinch the corners of the horse's mouth and put constant pressure on the bars and tongue. The width of the horse's mouth at the corners determines the width of the bit to be used. Five inches is an average snaffle width for an adult mouth. Ponies and fine-muzzled or young horses require narrower bits; warmbloods and draft crosses may need wider ones.

Buckling the headstall too short can cause the snaffle to pinch skin against the premolars and/or to exert constant pressure on the skin at the corners of the mouth as well as on the poll. This quickly leads to dullness and should be avoided.

Adjusting the headstall too long allows the bit to be positioned too low in the mouth and causes problems similar to those caused by the overly wide bit. Western trainers generally hang a snaffle lower in the horse's mouth than do their English counterparts. This is based on the theory that the Western horse is asked to find a comfortable place to carry the bit on his own (photo 99).

With a relatively loose headstall, the Western snaffle is free to move to several areas of the horse's bars. An upward pull on the reins will activate the area near the premolars. A backward pull acts more on the central area of the bars. This produces vertical flexion. Some of the maneuvers required in a Western snaffle-bit class, such as halts from a lope, prompt backs, and rollbacks, require a low head and vertical flexion using light contact and loose reins.

The English horse, on the other hand, is usually ridden with a more steady contact. To prevent a slight movement of the rider's hand from creating unwanted movement of the bit in the horse's mouth, the English snaffle is usually adjusted higher in the horse's mouth than the Western snaffle, generally leaving about two wrinkles at the corners of the mouth. The Western snaffle is often adjusted so there is only one wrinkle in the corner of the mouth, and sometimes no wrinkle at all.

Often a noseband is used with a snaffle bit. In general, a noseband prevents the horse from avoiding the action of the bit by keeping his mouth closed and stabilizing the position of the bit, which also encourages him to keep his tongue under the bit. While nosebands do not encourage mouthing of the bit, which is desirable in the young horse, they do decrease evaporation of saliva by keeping the mouth shut. Proper adjustment depends on the style of the noseband, but care must be exercised not to exert undue pressure on the soft cartilage of the horse's nose. Most nosebands are designed to apply pressure to the nasal bone and the chin groove.

The side-pieces of the snaffle may be rings of various sizes and shapes, or prongs called spoons or cheeks. The smaller the rings, the greater the chance that the snaffle could be pulled laterally through the horse's mouth. Using a noseband, **bit guard**s, or a **curb strap** can prevent this.

To avoid pinching skin in the corners of the mouth, most eggbutt or D-ring snaffles are constructed with the swivel mechanism located in a place on the ring that does not contact lip skin. Loose-ring snaffles or bradoons *can* create irritation, which may lead to a

99. *Properly fitted D-ring snaffle on a two-year-old. Note snaps on the headstall for quick changing of bits.*

sore on the corners of the lips. Bit guards can help alleviate this problem. Reduce the chances of pinching your horse by assuring that his bit is properly fitted and stabilized.

A full-cheek snaffle comes with a blunt prong (spoon) both above and below the mouthpiece of the bit. Half-cheek snaffles, traditionally used for driving, have either a spoon above or below the bit, but not both. Do not confuse spoons with shanks. Spoons provide added lateral persuasion; reins do not attach to them. When a rider pulls a left rein, the spoons pushing on the right side of the horse's face emphasize that the rider wants to turn left.

Behavior in a Snaffle.   A young horse in a snaffle bit reacts very differently than an older, schooled stablemate. The two-year-old usually carries his head high with his nose out. In this position the bit rests on and communicates almost entirely with the corners of the horse's mouth. The young horse will roll the bit around with his tongue, chew on it, and open his mouth as he tries to spit it out. These behaviors will decrease as he gradually accepts the bit and allows it to rest on his bars. If they resurface in an intensified form, you may need to solicit your veterinarian's help with dental care (see Chapter 11).

Sometimes a horse will put his tongue over the bit. He may be trying to find a comfortable place for the tongue, or he may be trying to avoid the pressure of the bit. This can develop into a very perplexing and serious problem. If your horse does this, try changing him to a wider bit or one that allows him more room for his tongue. You can also buckle the headstall tighter to discourage this habit from forming (photo 100).

Leading with the Bridle

Once the bridle has become part of your horse's daily working gear, there will be circumstances where you must lead him in it (photo 101). It is incorrect to lead the horse with the reins held collectively like a lead rope attached to a halter. Instead, you should begin building useful associations between signals on the snaffle and elementary maneuvers.

Hold the reins in your right hand a few inches from the bit, under the horse's jaw, and separate the reins with your index finger. Hold the end of the reins in your left hand. With your right hand, give

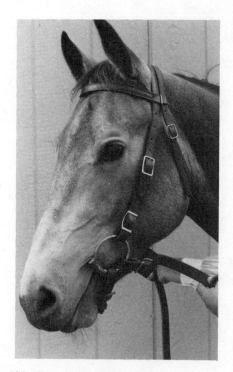

100. For a horse that tries to put his tongue over the bit, the headstall is shortened.

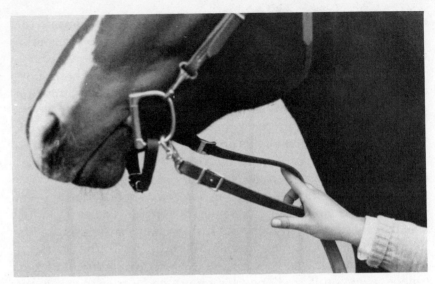

101. When leading with the bridle, treat each rein separately when turning.

appropriate cues to your horse, momentarily letting go of one rein while applying pressure with the other. A turn to the right, for example, is accomplished by dropping the left rein and lightly pulling the right rein out to the right. You should still position yourself between your horse's head and shoulder. You may want to carry a longe whip in your left hand along with the end of the reins to aid with impulsion. You do not want to get ahead of your horse and pull on the reins; this accomplishes nothing.

Introducing the Surcingle or Saddle

Finding a surcingle that will fit the girth of a long yearling or two-year-old can be somewhat difficult, but choices are usually available in web and leather. It is essential for long-reining later on to choose a surcingle with large loops or rings on the top so that the driving lines will flow freely.

Introducing the young horse to the pressure of a girth via a surcingle or saddle should be a separate lesson held in the confines of a training pen. With your horse haltered and hobbled, first review sacking-out procedures. Then let your horse smell and inspect the surcingle or saddle (photo 102). When he seems unafraid, place the

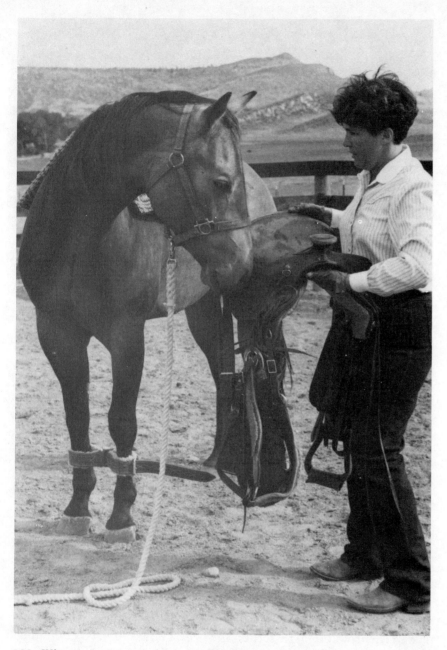

102. *When it is time to add the saddle, proceed as if it is an extension of the "sacking out" lesson. Let the horse inspect it.*

103. Lift the saddle gently onto the horse's back.

saddle gently in position (photo 103). Peak the saddle blanket in the gullet to prevent pressure on the withers. Using an assistant if necessary, fasten the girth(s) or cinches snugly. Be sure the cinches are tight enough to prevent the saddle from slipping under the horse's belly if he runs or bucks. With a Western saddle, always fasten the front cinch first, then the breast collar (if used), and finally the rear cinch. When removing the saddle, unbuckle these in the reverse order.

Let your horse stand hobbled and saddled for a few moments until he has relaxed somewhat. Then remove his hobbles and walk him forward, taking care to stand well to his side at the shoulder in the event he lunges forward in a reaction to the girth pressure. After walking him for several minutes, trot him in hand or on the longe line to let him become accustomed to the saddle. Check the cinches periodically to ensure their safe adjustment.

Side Reins

In preparation for **long-reining** and riding, you should begin teaching your young horse to carry himself and further develop his **longitudinal** and lateral flexion by attaching side reins from either his halter or bit to a surcingle or saddle once he has accepted the pressure of the surcingle or saddle. Start by letting him wear the bridle during longe lessons with very loose side-rein attachments. Side reins often have elasticized inserts to allow more natural movement to the horse's head and neck (photo 104). Over several

104. Allow the horse to become accustomed to light bit contact with elasticized side reins.

lessons, you should gradually adjust these side reins to create more contact with the horse's mouth; this helps him learn balance and **rounding**. Side reins are also good for stretching, conditioning, and suppling your horse.

You have many choices of position in which to affix the side reins to a saddle or surcingle. The idea is to attach the reins at a level which approximates a straight line between the horse's mouth and where the rider's hands will eventually be. To reach that stage, however, you may have to vary the side reins' position on the surcingle or saddle to accommodate the carriage of your horse's head. On a circle twenty meters (sixty-six feet) in diameter, the pressure on both reins should be virtually even. Tying the inside rein shorter asks the horse for a degree of bend in the head and neck inappropriate for that circle size. Leaving the outside rein too loose may cause your horse to lean on the inside rein because he cannot find the outside rein. This will make him fall to the inside of the circle.

LONG-REINING

Equipment:
Two 35-foot driving lines.
Stirrup hobble rope or strap for fastening stirrups together under the horse's belly.

Long-reining (also known as ground-driving) has similar benefits to longeing and furthermore relates the signals for gait transitions, turns, and halts more specifically to the signals of the reins. It can cure a horse who turns to face the trainer or one who cuts off part of the circle since the outside line keeps the horse straight and on the track.

There are four styles of working a horse from the ground with long reins:
1. *English:* (Also known as Western ground-driving): Using reins run through the lower rings of a **bitting rig** or the stirrups of a Western or English saddle, you drive the horse either ahead of you or around in a circle. In the latter situation, the outside rein comes to your hands from around the hocks. In both instances

105. *After adjusting the reins, secure them with two half hitches on the saddle horn.*

106. *This two-year-old is carrying a saddle and bridle while being longed with a halter.*

the stirrups are hobbled securely together under the horse's belly to prevent them from swinging out to the sides during turns or resistances (photos 115 and 116).

2. *Danish:* Using reins run through the top **terrets** of a bitting rig and then across the middle of the horse's back, you walk alongside the horse as you school him on light contact to movements containing high levels of difficulty.

3. *French:* Using reins run through a collar and the side terrets of a bitting rig, you drive the horse forward from the rear. This method emphasizes a higher head and neck position reminiscent of French carriage horses.

107. Sisal rope lines have more weight and sting and can potentially cause rope burns. They are shown here with a D-ring snaffle. The curb strap prevents the snaffle from being pulled through the horse's mouth in the event of a mishap.

4. *Viennese:* Although the horse wears a bitting rig or decorated saddle pad, the reins do not pass through terrets but go directly from the bit to your hands. This method is usually only used to exhibit an already very well-trained horse.

The English method of long-reining is the best method to use when introducing the exercise to the two-year-old. It allows you to gain obedience from a young horse by using mechanical leverage. Because of the low rein position, however, overuse of this type of driving may lead to a low head carriage and overbending at the jaw and poll. Once your horse is obedient and controllable, you may want to advance to the Danish style of driving, which does not present this problem.

When long-reining your horse, you do not usually carry a whip. Your reins and voice are the cues for impulsion. To move your horse forward or over, "cast a wave" in the driving line, aiming at a particular hindquarter, shoulder, or side. It can not be overemphasized that this "giving" gesture never should result in a pull on the bit in the horse's mouth.

Driving lines come in a wide range of materials, which will vary in feel and response. They constitute your primary aids when long-reining, and so must be both lightweight to handle and substantial enough for control. Some web driving lines are far too light and limp to pitch a wave that will have impact on a horse who is twenty feet away. Sisal rope lines have a good snap and firmness but can be heavy on the horse's mouth and rider's hands and can cause friction burns if a fight ensues (photo 107). Leather lines, although quite expensive, are ideal for long-reining (photo 108).

For safety, all long-reining should take place in a safe enclosure (photo 109). The first lesson usually entails tacking up, affixing the lines (photo 110), stepping a safe distance behind the horse, and asking him to walk forward. If possible, have an assistant at the horse's head to give him added confidence and help prevent problems. The "plow-driving" phase of the English/Western method gives your young horse a chance to feel your hands through the lines in a balanced position. At this stage, the lines do not cross a moving part of his body, and thus are relatively stable and non-irritating (photo 111).

108. Leather surcingle, leather driving lines, and smooth-mouth hunt snaffle with figure-eight noseband. Training for ground manners pays off the first time the horse is tacked up for driving. This yearling demonstrates "whoa" so a photo can be taken.

109. The round pen is a fine place for ground-driving lessons.

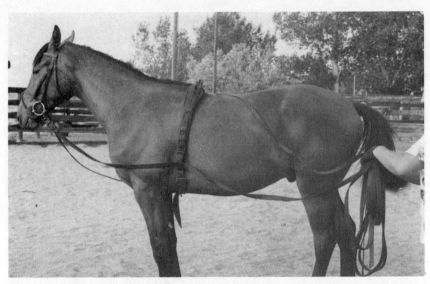

110. *As the trainer takes the lines, the horse remains halted until asked to walk forward as in longeing or in-hand work. If the lines passed through the top terrets of the surcingle, this would be an example of the Danish style of long-reining. For the English style, the off line will be moved to the right side.*

111. *The trainer begins driving at a safe distance to the rear. The horse is asked to walk calmly forward.*

Once you have taught your horse the walk (photo 112) and halt (photo 113), you can step to the side of the horse and send him around you as in longeing (photos 114 and 115). If you took the time earlier to familiarize your young horse with ropes, he should not be alarmed when he feels the outside line on his hocks.

You should trot you horse in circles and figure-eights as an introduction to the give and take between the left and right lines. It is important in a change of direction that you allow the rein of the old direction to give way to the rein of the new direction, thereby avoiding conflicting signals.

Although it is possible to canter a horse on the long lines, you must be sure to have an adequate length of line (a minimum of thirty-five feet) to go around the horse's body while allowing

112. *The trainer asks the horse to arc left by giving a slight pull on the left line and releasing the right line.*

113. *The halt.*

114. *Gradually the trainer steps to the inside of the pen and begins to send the horse around in a circle as in longeing. Sisal lines are in use.*

115. *Tracking quietly at the trot, this two-year-old gains experience with the snaffle. Leather lines are in use.*

enough line for the horse to canter a large circle. For many two-year-olds this is too advanced a maneuver; however, it depends on the horse and your goals for him.

Backing is best introduced from the plow-driving position, which helps ensure straightness in the maneuver. All rein cues should involve intermittent or vibrating pressure on the bit. With backing, this lesson is paramount as steady pressure seems to encourage resistance. When teaching this "**rein back**" maneuver to the dressage prospect, do not overdo it, otherwise the horse might experience some confusion in later training when introduced to lateral movements.

116. With the stirrups hobbled under the horse's belly, the lines are passed through them. The horse wears protective boots in case of an imbalance. Note: In this photo, the end of the stirrup-hobble rope has flipped on top of the left driving line. It is not attached.

If you use a saddle to long-rein, hobble the stirrups securely under the horse's belly.

Some of the common problems and hazards of long-reining and their solutions are the following:

• *Problem:* The horse does the "spaghetti twirl" by turning and facing you, becoming frightened, and continuing to spin until he is unmercifully tangled in the lines.

Solution: This can be a real setback, complete with friction burns, so must be avoided at all costs. Properly familiarize your horse with the equipment and use progressive stages of driving styles. Keep even contact on the lines, paying special attention to the inside line. Take care not to exert tense, unyielding pressure on it. Rather, use the inside line occasionally to push the horse (with a pop to the hip) over to the outside line. Assert the driving aids (lines and voice) early.

- *Problem:* You drop a line.

   Solution: This can happen if the lines are too short, if the pen is too large, or if you are inexperienced. The horse's reaction to this should be inconsequential if he has been properly sacked out and knows "whoa." Review these lessons if he gets upset.
- *Problem:* You get tangled in the lines.

   Solution: Some professionals prefer to carry the lines in a separate coil in each hand; others let the excess line trail behind them. The method of choice depends on how far away the horse is working from you and subsequently how much line is left. If tangling occurs, a foot in a loop is dangerous. Never let too much excess line drag on the ground.

- *Problem:* The horse overflexes and gets behind the bit.

   Solution: Check to see whether the lines may be too heavy, your hands too heavy, or the bit too severe. Be sure you are generating enough impulsion.

Once the two-year-old has learned all of the previous lessons, he can be turned out for the winter. In the spring, you should review these lessons for a few weeks. Then you can begin mounted training.

The Two-Year-Old

The Author Training a Foal

NINE

Characteristics of the Successful Horse Trainer

A trainer should have a broad base of equine knowledge, sound reasoning abilities, a mechanical aptitude, and an inquiring mind. Training requires innovative techniques and sensitivity, not brute strength. It flourishes with organization, progressive planning, and well-thought-out procedures.

It is essential for a trainer to like horses and all the duties associated with them. An even temper and a healthy ego help develop the consistency necessary for success. It is good to have high personal standards, be goal-oriented, and be willing to learn. A self-disciplined individual usually produces high yields. A good trainer is not afraid of the unpredictable nature of the horse but at the same time has a healthy respect for the occupational hazards.

A creative, imaginative person who is content to work alone and is a good self-evaluator will have an easier time designing training programs and following through with them. A trainer should have good instincts and a positive attitude to help figure out problems and keep things moving in a progressive fashion. The professional trainer must like to deal with people as well as horses, must be honest, and have a high code of ethics.

A trainer must be healthy and moderately strong, with supple and durable neck, shoulders, back, knees, and ankles. Good diet and exercise will make a good trainer better.

The trainer must also have time available for training. If there are constraints on the trainer's schedule, her performance will suffer. There is more to training than riding a horse and much of it entails hard work.

133

Part Three

MANAGEMENT

ТEN

Working with Your Professionals

The veterinarian, farrier, and trainer offer valuable assistance to the horse owner who raises and trains young horses. It does not pay to alienate these people with undesirable working conditions, false expectations, or unruly horses. A good relationship is based on preparation, consideration, and professional respect.

THE VETERINARIAN

The value of establishing a herd health program, whether it is for one horse or many, is multifold. A week-by-week plan designed by your veterinarian will give you a guideline to follow throughout the year. It will prevent or reduce the potential for infectious disease outbreaks, eliminate or reduce the damage caused to the horse by adult and migrating internal parasites, and help you to evaluate your nutritional program. It will also establish a routine of scheduled visits by the veterinarian to monitor all phases of health, growth, and development of your horse, and to examine the horse for incidental abnormalities and deficiencies.

It is a great help to the veterinarian when the horse owner accepts certain responsibilities. The following list recommends ways you can make your relationship with your veterinarian a good one.
• Make your routine appointments well in advance.
• Have horses ready, clean, and quiet.
• Train your horses to accept twitches, stud chains, and leg restraints.
• Use strong halters and lead ropes of the proper size for all horses to be treated.
• Accustom your horse to having his ears, lips, and head handled.

137

- Ask your veterinarian where he (or she) wants you to stand, if he wants the horse tied or held, and how else you may be of assistance.
- Have a safe, strong place to tie your horse.
- If you have to talk, do so in calm, quiet tones.
- Prepare an appropriate place for the veterinarian to work: somewhere clean, light, and safe. Familiarize the horse ahead of time to being handled in this area by doing something pleasurable there such as grooming.
- Become familiar with first-aid principles, especially wound care.
- Offer to pay for consultation before becoming involved in long conversations.
- Ask your veterinarian to develop a health plan for your horses and then follow his advice.
- Have checkbook handy and pay for services when they are performed unless other arrangements are customary.
- Remember that veterinarians have private lives. They look forward to evenings and weekends, too. Do not call them during their nonworking hours unless you have a serious emergency.

THE FARRIER

Good farriers are scarce. They are usually strong in body and mind, educated and innovative, patient and firm. In addition to keen reflexes, technical knowledge, and the eye of an artist, a successful farrier should have a highly developed sense of the three H's: sense of humor, sense of human, and of course, sense of horse. If your farrier fits this description, hang on to him. Here's how.

First of all, get to know your farrier's preference for appointments. Does he like to schedule you for a definite appointment six weeks in advance? If so, do either of you have to phone to confirm the appointment the day before? Or does your farrier prefer to have you call him as you need him? If so, when should you call? One week ahead, or one day ahead? Scheduling is the most common problem in getting continuous farrier service. It is often best to make a routine appointment every six weeks.

If you have a great number of horses or if your horses differ greatly in their shoeing schedules, perhaps you could arrange to have your farrier come on a particular morning each week unless otherwise notified.

When you are on the phone with your farrier, have an accurate list for him of what you need done, e.g., two to shoe all around, three broodmares and one yearling to trim. If your needs happen to change before the farrier arrives, have the courtesy to call him so he can adjust the rest of his day's schedule accordingly.

Mention in advance any special problems that your horses may have so that your farrier can be sure to have custom supplies on hand when he visits. Some farrier's rigs look like a veritable store with a huge inventory of shoes, pads, nails, and accessories all pigeonholed and categorized.

Before the farrier arrives, collect all the horses he will be working on and tie them where he will be working or put them in stalls or small pens that are conveniently located to the working area. Each horse should have a well-fitted halter and lead rope.

There should be an appropriate place for your farrier to work. It is important that it have a secure place to tie the horses at a level above the height of their withers. The work area should be well lighted, uncluttered, and level. Some horseshoers prefer to work on a concrete slab.

Although direct sunlight helps your farrier see what he is doing, hot summer sun can be extremely fatiguing. Try to provide some shade and shelter and both your farrier and your horse will be happier.

If your horses have come out of muddy lots, groom their shoulder and hindquarter areas. Also, wipe or scrape the mud off hooves rather than hosing them off. Clean, dry hooves are much better for the farrier to work on. Make things nice for your farrier and chances are he will respond in kind.

Your horses should all be convinced that they can stand on three legs. They should support their own weight, not lean.

Now here are some **Dos** and **Don'ts** for the actual farrier visit.

DO offer to hold young stock if it is their first time or two being trimmed.

DON'T feel offended if your offer is rejected.

DO have plenty of fly repellent on hand.

DON'T wait until your farrier's visit to acquaint your horse with a spray bottle.

DO tell your horseshoer the name, age, and use of each animal, but

DON'T expect your farrier to carry on a conversation. He is there for one reason alone: to provide a professional service.

DO pay attention to your horse's behavior, but

DON'T take your nervous horse for a walk down the gravel driveway on freshly trimmed feet while the farrier is shaping a shoe.

DO discuss stable management and hoof care with your farrier. Ask him about the symptoms of problems he sees in your horse's feet and follow his recommendations to remedy them.

DON'T expect miracles in one visit. The farrier's rasp is not magic. It cannot cure cracks, founder, conformation flaws, or thrush overnight. Only by working together can you gradually achieve improvement.

DO have your payment in full ready before he leaves or make sure he has your address if he prefers billing you.

DON'T make him ask.

DO ask him how long until the next shoeing.

DO offer him water for washing and drinking.

THE TRAINER

When working with a trainer either by monthly contract or periodic lessons, abandon yourself to her theories and principles until you either know more than she does or have found another trainer that more appropriately suits your needs.

Make your goals clear and be careful not to create false expectations for your horse. A good trainer will give you an honest evaluation of your horse's potential. Listen to her and keep an open mind.

Be sure financial arrangements have been made clear before you commit to a long-term training situation. Generally the monthly fee quoted by trainers includes training, board, feed, and bedding. Farrier and veterinary bills are an additional expense to be borne by the owner.

Occasionally you may wish to check your horse's progress while he is in training. Be courteous. Don't arrive unannounced or your trainer may feel forced to juggle her schedule. If the trainer is busy working another horse, do not interrupt. Long talks during the trainer's working day rob other clients of her precious time.

When you begin lessons with your horse, arrive promptly and be prepared with appropriate dress and equipment. Listen carefully and follow your trainer's instructions to the best of your ability. Save questions about theory for after the horse has been put away and be prepared to pay adequately for your trainer's time talking with you.

ELEVEN

Veterinary Care and Health Management

CARE OF THE NEWBORN FOAL

Once the foal is born he begins an important adaptive process. He must make an adjustment from the security of the womb to the noises, lights, and other experiences of the world. Ninety-five percent of foaling mares need no help. Foaling often occurs not only without incident, but without invitation. Following the expulsive phase of parturition, the foal often lies with his hind legs still in the vagina and partially enveloped in the placenta. The mare and foal customarily nicker to each other while in this position. Important bonding is taking place as the foal registers the smells and sounds of his species. In addition, two or more pints of blood, which are in the umbilical vessels and placenta, may be transferred to the foal during this time. The pair should be undisturbed until they are ready to get up. Within minutes of birth, the normal foal will raise his head, assume the sternal recumbent position (see page 10) and begin moving his lips in the sucking reflex.

When either the mare or foal stands, the umbilical cord will usually break at its weakest spot about two inches from the foal's abdominal wall. If possible, you should immediately drench the navel stump in iodine to prevent bacterial invasion.

For the next hour, most foals struggle awkwardly to stand. It is best to resist the temptation to help; let the foal stand on his own. As the foal takes uneven steps, he often bumps into stall walls and other objects as he gradually learns coordination. Within one to two hours, the foal should locate the mare's udder, begin nursing, and ingest colostrum, the protein and antibody-rich first milk produced by the mare for about twenty-four hours after parturition. Since the foal is born with no immune protection, it is essential that

142

he receives the colostral immunoglobulins from the dam during the first eighteen hours after birth. His small intestine is capable of absorbing the large molecule proteins containing colostral antibodies for only up to twenty-four hours.

The foal needs to rid his digestive system of the waste products that accumulated in the colon during the last several months of his development. The fetal manure or meconium may be black, stiff, and tarlike or range in color from brown to near orange-yellow. Should the foal exhibit signs of straining in an effort to expel the meconium, you can give him a disposable human enema at body temperature to soften and lubricate the meconium and to assist in relieving the condition. Colts experience retained meconium much more frequently than do fillies. Once the foal begins to digest the mare's milk, the newborn's manure will soften and turn yellowish in color.

The foal alternates between eating and sleeping with a little walking interspersed. Ideally, you should provide a quiet, clean, comfortable place for him to acclimate to the outside world. It is good to have your veterinarian give the new foal a checkup the day after he is born. This will often identify abnormalities, congenital defects, or early **septicemic** signs that might otherwise be unobserved. Keeping an eye on the progress of the foal and his behavior in the first days will give you added assurance that he is normal and will enjoy a healthy development.

DAILY EXAMINATION FOR HORSES OF ALL AGES

It is important for you to know the norm for each of your horses so you have a means of evaluating deviations. Taking the temperature, pulse, and respiration once or twice a day for a few days and recording the numbers will provide a valuable reference point. Mean resting temperature is about 100 degrees Fahrenheit for an adult horse with a range of one degree above or below. You can easily insert a thermometer lubricated with petroleum jelly or saliva into the rectum; leave it there for two to three minutes before taking a reading (photo 117).

Resting adult pulse rates vary between 35 and 40 beats per

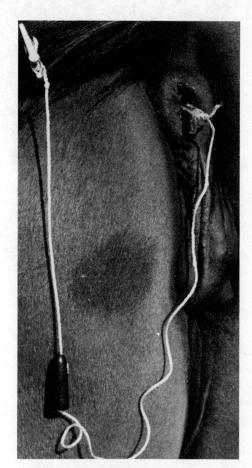

117. A rectal thermometer on a string with an alligator clip for the tail. Note the misshapen vulva.

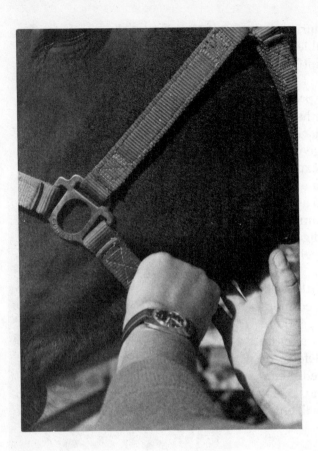

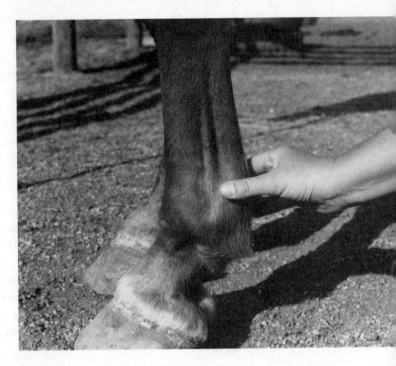

118. Pulse may be easily be taken at the jaw

119. or at the fetlock.

minute, while a young horse's is considerably higher. A two-week-old foal's pulse rate can be as high as 100 beats per minute, a four-week-old's 70 beats, a yearling's 45 to 60 beats, and a two-year-old's 40 to 50 beats per minute. You can easily take pulse rates both at the maxillary artery of the lower jaw (photo 118) and at the meta-carpal artery at the rear of the fetlock (photo 119). Pulse rates go up with excitement, pain, nervousness, elevated body temperature, shock, infectious disease, and exercise.

A horse's normal respiration rate is 12 to 25 breaths per minute. The foal may be at the high end of this scale. One breath is measured as one inhalation and one exhalation. The ratio of the pulse to respiration is often a more significant measure of stress than the actual individual figures are. Depending on the horse's age, his normal resting ratios will range from 4:1 to 2:1. If the relationship is 1:1 or 1:2, a horse is suffering oxygen deprivation. This inversion indicates stress.

The pinch test is a quick and easy subjective way to measure dehydration. If you pick up a fold of skin in the shoulder area and then release it, it should return to its flat position within a second. If the skin remains peaked for two to three seconds, it may indicate some degree of body-fluid loss. A standing "tent" of a five to ten-second duration indicates moderate to severe dehydration. Blood tests can be given to determine the actual degree of dehydration that the horse may have.

Inspecting the mucous membranes for a bright pink color and appropriate moisture gives you information on the horse's overall health and the function of his circulatory system. Roll back the horse's upper lip and exert firm thumb pressure on the gum for two seconds. When you remove your thumb, a circular white spot will remain. Within one second, the spot should return to its original color; this is the capillary refill time. If it takes five to ten seconds, your horse is showing signs of circulatory impairment. Extended capillary refill time is often seen in horses with severe colic and/or in shock.

Careful palpation and visual examination of a horse's legs, particularly after strenuous work, often reveals swelling, heat, and pain, which are indications of inflammation. You should make it a point to run your hands down your horse's legs to check them on a daily basis.

If your horse's muscle tone changes drastically from his norm, it could indicate a serious situation. Rigid contractions can be signs of overall metabolic stress, such as **tying up**. Flaccid muscles may indicate depressed central nervous system activity or shock.

PARASITE MANAGEMENT

Allowing the growing and developing horse ample room to exercise and graze also adds to his overall health by decreasing exposure to parasite reinfestation. Although it is virtually impossible to have a parasite-free horse, management can go a long way in keeping intestinal parasites under control. Daily removal of feces from eating areas, pasture rotation, and regular deworming are recommended. During the late summer, bot flies (gasterophilus) lay their yellowish eggs on the horse's leg hairs. You should remove the eggs daily with a **bot block** for optimum bot control.

Routine administration of paste dewormers is a cost-effective means of parasite control (photos 120–123). It is recommended that you rotate the classes of dewormers you use on your horse since parasites can develop a resistance to a particular chemical. In

120. *Before deworming, it may be necessary to clean the horse's mouth of feed. Several syringes full of water will do the trick.*

121. *Deworming the foal can be a one-person operation if the youngster has had sufficient handling.*

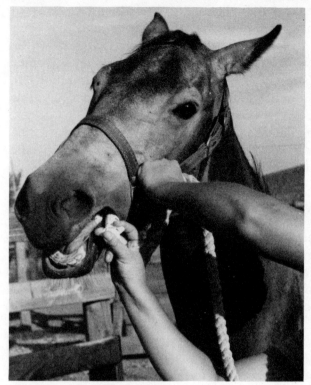

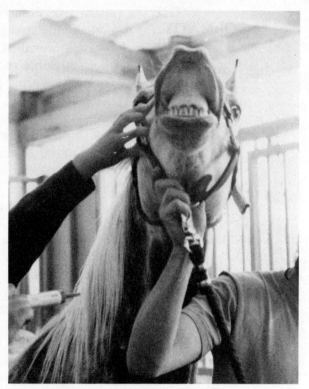

122. The tube should be inserted far back on the horse's tongue.

123. The medication may make the horse exhibit the Flehmen response.

any deworming program, if a horse does not seem to respond to treatment, you should have a fecal examination performed, being sure to provide your veterinarian or laboratory with a fresh manure sample. Some deworming products are more specific for certain parasites than others, so ask your veterinarian for advice in setting up a parasite-control program.

Foals need to be dewormed once each month until they are six months old, then every six weeks until they are one year old, and then every two months with the rest of the mature horses. Young horses have a greater susceptibility to roundworm (ascarid) infestation than adults. They are also apt to suffer from bloodworms (strongyles), which do the most permanent damage as they migrate through the horse's tissues, and pinworms (oxyuris), which can cause troublesome anal itch. Therefore, you should target your horse's medication for roundworms, bloodworms, and pinworms every deworming and for bots during the late fall and winter months. Some suckling and weanling foals need to be dewormed for threadworms (strongyloides) until they develop immunity to them at about six months of age. Thiabendazole is effective in this case.

A sample deworming schedule and drug reference chart can be found in the Appendix. Be sure to ask your veterinarian for specific recommendations for your farm.

IMMUNIZATIONS

Most equine vaccinations will be given to your horse by your veterinarian during his routine spring and fall visits. Few young horses object to properly administered **intramuscular injections**. If your horse is afraid, usually this fear comes from insufficient handling prior to his first vaccination or from the fact that the administrator of the vaccination is inexperienced. Unless you have a great deal of experience, seek the help of a professional rather than take a chance giving the injections yourself.

Commonly, horses are vaccinated each year in the spring for protection against tetanus, influenza, Eastern and Western **encephalomyelitis**, and **rhinopneumonitis**. In addition, it may be recommended in your area to vaccinate for rabies, **strangles**, or Venezuelan sleeping sickness. Confer with your veterinarian to determine your needs. A sample vaccination schedule for the young horse can be found in the Appendix.

BLOOD TESTS

Blood tests are performed to determine metabolic imbalances, degenerative and disease conditions, musculoskeletal abnormalities, general and specific levels of immunity, and blood types. Expensive blood workups are only indicated if they are preceded by a thorough veterinary examination revealing clinical signs requiring further information.

Blood is comprised of a cellular component made up of red blood cells (erythrocytes), white blood cells (leukocytes), and platelets (thrombocytes) in a fluid medium (plasma). After coagulation, the noncellular portion is referred to as serum. The average healthy horse's blood at rest is 40 percent cells and 60 percent fluid. Blood supplies oxygen to cells, removes waste products, and provides a line of defense against infectious invaders.

The effectiveness of the immune system can be measured quantitatively and qualitatively by testing the serum protein levels. When a horse is exposed to a disease-causing organism (antigen), either by direct contact or through a vaccine, he forms an active immunity. The antigenic stimulation precipitates antibody formation. The serum antibody **titer**, or concentration, is a good indicator of immunologic protection. The presence of specific antigens can also be determined by testing the serum.

The Coggins test is a diagnostic test used to reveal a prior immune system response to equine infectious anemia. (EIA). This agar gel immunodiffusion test developed by Dr. LeRoy Coggins checks for the existence of serum immunoglobulins by exposing a particular horse's blood to the EIA virus. A positive test indicates the horse has previously come in direct contact with the disease-causing organism and as a result already has antibodies, which in this instance is not good news. Since this disease is very contagious, horses testing positive must be quarantined or destroyed. Newer tests for EIA are being developed and research continues in an effort to develop a vaccine.

When clinical signs indicate your horse has a disease, you may want to obtain total and differential white blood cell counts. The number and proportion of the five major types of leukocytes give clues to the type of infection, the duration of the affliction, and potential upcoming emergencies.

Blood typing is useful for identification, disease prediction, and selection of transfusion donors. At birth, a horse possesses certain antigenic factors on his red blood cells. These factors are responsible for the initiation of antibody formation and are not affected by environmental influences. Subsequently, they do not change throughout the life of the individual. Since there are ten possible blood types in horses and many antigenic factor combinations and positions, it has been suggested that there could be over one million blood genotypes among the various breeds.

By process of elimination, blood typing can solve at least 70 percent of all paternity cases involving two sires or dams. Testing can not prove a horse to be the true parent, but it can show which horse could not possibly be the parent in question. Research is in progress to develop positive tests for parentage identification.

Blood typing may prove necessary for the identification of compatible donors if a horse needs to receive more than one blood transfusion. Little problem is usually encountered with a single untyped whole blood transfusion.

Fitness is sometimes measured by determining the number and/or size of red blood cells (RBCs). Another common measure of fitness is the percentage of whole blood that is comprised of cells: the packed cell volume (PCV) or hematocrit. Since red blood cells, and specifically their hemoglobin, are responsible for oxygen transfer, a measure of the hemoglobin concentration (oxygen-carrying capacity) is thought to indicate athletic potential.

Blood counts can be inaccurate and misinterpreted because of the action of the horse's spleen. At rest, 30 to 60 percent of the horse's red blood cells are stored in the spleen. A spongelike, smooth muscle regulated by the autonomic nervous system, the spleen responds to adrenal hormones in "fight or flight" situations. Muscular exertion, excitement, fright, or apprehension triggers the spleen to dump red blood cells; in seconds, trillions of RBCs are sent into the blood stream to accommodate the horse's sudden need for oxygen. As the horse gradually returns to rest, the cells are soaked up again by the spleen. This phenomenon makes the resting packed cell volume much lower than the working percentage.

The best time for taking a sample to determine a working PCV is within thirty seconds of strenuous exercise. A working PCV of 52 to 58 percent is optimum for a performance horse. The resting PCV in the performance horse may range from 34 to 44 percent. Such counts indicate adequate cells for oxygen transfer but not enough to cause sludging. When there are too many cells in too little plasma the circulatory system is taxed as it attempts to keep the blood thin enough to pump through the body at the rapid rate required during performance.

If you are measuring a resting PCV, it is imperative that you procure the sample quickly and calmly to prevent splenic contraction. A sample taken from a nervous horse or by an inexperienced technician may give a falsely high resting PCV.

DENTAL CARE

Horses have two main groups of teeth: twelve incisors at the front of the mouth and twenty-four to twenty-eight molars (or cheek teeth) at the back of the mouth. The first twelve to sixteen molars are often referred to as premolars; the last twelve are called molars.

Through evolutionary processes, the first premolar (or wolf tooth) has served a progressively less important function, and so has diminished in size and may be absent in a horse. If it is present, it is usually rudimentary in size. When the permanent second premolar erupts at 2½ years, it may push the temporary second premolar out of the way. The variability in the number of premolars (twelve to sixteen) a horse has is explained by the presence or absence of from one to four wolf teeth. Some horses have no wolf teeth, some lose them in the shedding process of their second premolars, and some have had them extracted (see illustration on page 152).

In male horses, canines will appear in the interdental space at about four years of age and be fully developed at five. The canines, also called bridle teeth or tushes, erupt nearer the incisors. Canines can also be present in mares, in which case they are usually small buds.

Commonly, tooth problems are first noticed when there is a change in the eating habits and condition of a horse. If a horse drops wads of hay or grain from his mouth in a frustrated attempt at chewing, he probably needs help. If he holds his head extended or at an odd angle during his meals, he may be trying to position the feed in the only comfortable corner of his mouth. If his water pail is full of hay stems or unchewed grain, he may be drinking to moisten and soften his feed. Close inspection may reveal an undesirable mouth odor often associated with "caps" or as-yet-unexpelled temporary or "baby tooth" molars.

Even if a horse's eating habits and condition are normal, he may show signs of oral discomfort when being bridled or dewormed. The need for a dental checkup should not be ignored. Repeated bruising of mouth tissues from tooth problems can lead to scar tissue or chronic sores. Both are undesirable and unnecessary.

Subtle signs that things aren't quite right in the bridled horse's mouth may be an irritable expression in his ears or eyes as pressure is applied in a certain way on a rein. Tail swishing, although an

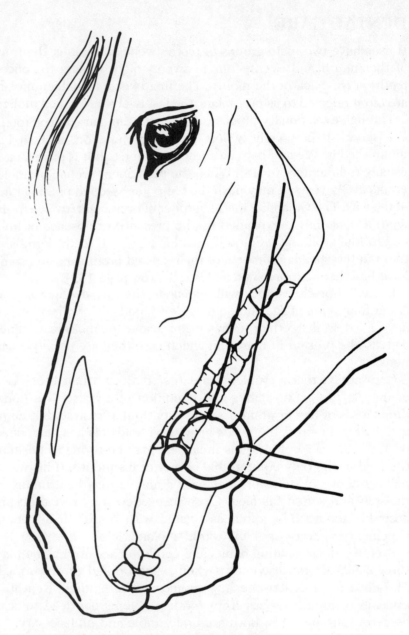

The Two-Year-Old Mouth with Snaffle Bit
Note the upper first premolar (wolf tooth)

indicator of many maladies, can be a substitute behavior for head shaking. If a horse has been taught not to shake his head, he looks for another outlet for his frustration.

When a horse has tooth problems, you may suddenly find him resistant to maneuvers to one direction. The horse may be willing to the right, but stiff and uncooperative to the left. If the problem affects teeth on both sides of the mouth, the horse may avoid contact with the bit altogether. He may do this by coming above the bit, that is, sticking his head up and out to keep the bit off his bars and tongue. Or he may overflex at the poll and drop behind the bit, letting the headstall suspend the bit in space somewhere in his mouth cavity.

If during bridling your horse tries to move his head away from you and swing his rump toward you or raises his head and pins back his ears, it's past time to get to the "root" of the problem (photos 124 and 125).

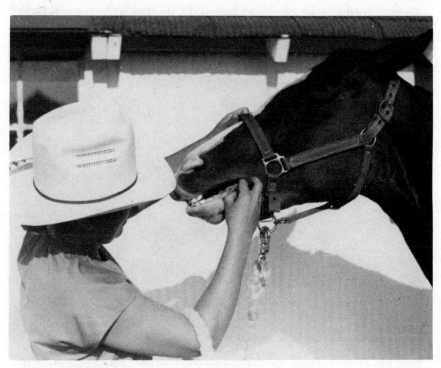

124. Periodically check the premolars for sharp edges.

There are five common procedures that can be performed by your veterinarian that will help maintain proper working order of your horse's mouth. They are canine filing, routine **floating**, wolf-tooth extraction, cap removal, and "putting on a snaffle mouth." All but the first one may be necessary for the young horse.

Routine floating is the process of filing off the sharp edges of the premolars and molars. The upper jaw of the horse is 30 percent wider than the lower jaw (illustration on facing page). As the horse grinds his feed in a somewhat side-to-side motion, he wears his molars and premolars unevenly. Sharp edges form on the outside (cheek surfaces) of the upper teeth and on the inside edges (tongue surfaces) of the lower teeth. Even a horse with normal dental conformation and on a regular ration can have these sharp edges.

At first the small lacerations on the tongue or cheek surfaces may merely bleed. However, as food debris collects, an infection can ensue and chronic sores can develop.

Sharp molars can be smoothed and rounded by various types of dental floats. Most veterinarians rasp the edges manually with files,

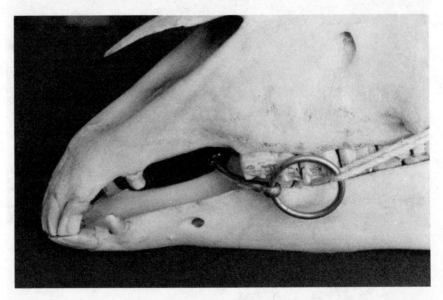

125. The second premolar can form a sharp overhanging shelf that may pinch skin between the bit and the horse's tooth.

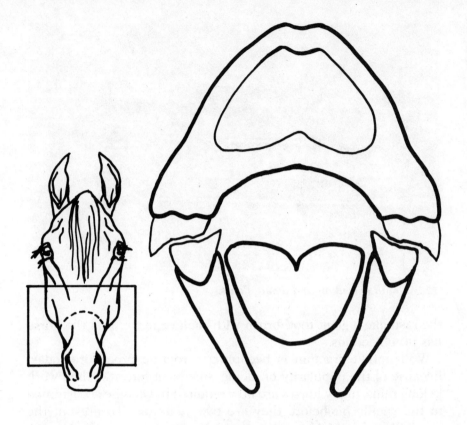

The Reason for Floating Teeth
*A cross-section of the upper and lower jaws at about the second premolar
position showing the sharp points that form on the cheek surfaces of the
upper molars and the tongue surfaces of the lower molars.*

much as the farrier does when shaping a rough hoof wall. The surfaces of the files are usually hard steel or carbide chips (photo 126).
Floating requires vigorous physical effort. A veterinarian can work
up quite a sweat from the exertion required to properly care for the
horse's teeth.

Some veterinarians float the horse's teeth while an assistant
holds the horse's tongue out to one side. Other practitioners use a
mouth speculum that looks like a V-shaped ramp and fits into one
side of the horse's mouth to wedge it open. Still others merely work

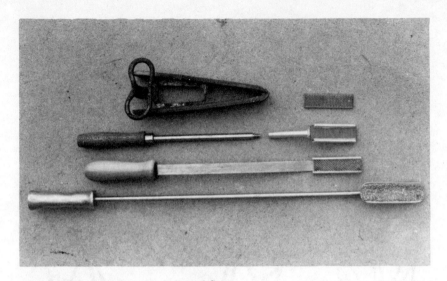

126. Mouth speculum and dental floats.

the rasp like a giant toothbrush with such expertise that the horse has no objections.

Wolf-tooth extraction is becoming a routine procedure today. Because of the popularity of racing, snaffle-bit futurities, and work in long reins, many horses are now required to become accustomed to the snaffle bit before they are two years old. To prevent the possibility of painful bumping or pinching when the snaffle is introduced to a youngster, it is often recommended that his wolf teeth be removed at about two years of age. Wolf teeth are found more commonly in the upper jaw, and their extraction is a minor, on-the-farm procedure. Depending upon the individual horse's nature and the facilities available, your veterinarian will probably perform the extraction using a tranquilizer and a local anesthetic. He may also use a twitch to ensure control. If you have stocks, your veterinarian may use them to help restrain your horse during the extraction.

The temporary, shallow-rooted milk teeth (caps) in the second and third premolar positions can be removed by your veterinarian when your horse is 3½ and 4½ respectively. If not removed, the cap sometimes hangs onto the permanent tooth as it erupts, or even worse, detaches only partially and rotates, lacerating the cheek.

Canines in the mature male horse rarely become long enough to interfere with chewing or acceptance of the bridle. If there is a problem, the conservative approach is to file or clip the tips off the canine teeth. If they are infected or grow at a rapid rate, you can elect to have them removed. Extraction is performed with the horse under general anesthesia.

Even with wolf teeth and caps removed and canines under control, there still is the possibility the horse will have discomfort with the bit. When one rein of the snaffle bit is pulled, lip skin can be caught between the bit and the overhanging shelf that is formed by the second premolar (photo 125). To ensure that any contact between skin, tooth, and bit is as safe as possible, many horse owners today ask their veterinarians to "put a snaffle mouth" on their horses. Besides the aforementioned procedures, this process involves rounding of the second premolar to add to the successful communication between the trainer's hand and the horse's mouth. The premolar is rounded from side to side as well as from top to bottom. This can be done with files, much as in floating. However, some veterinarians use a motorized burr to accomplish the same thing. Although the motor may alarm a young horse, it makes the veterinarian's job much easier.

HOOF CARE

Horses have evolved from a semi-arid environment, so their external hoof structures are well adapted to dryness. In fact, many hoof problems can be linked to excess external moisture and deficient internal moisture. Horses that are confined to stalls experience the worst of both evils (see illustration on page 158). Standing in manure, urine, and wet bedding softens the supporting structures of the foot, and the strong acids can decompose tissues and set the stage for further complications. Muddy lots are equally damaging. When the hoof gets wet, it expands, and when the mud dries around the hoof, it leaches precious internal moisture. This expansion and contraction on a daily basis can destroy the integrity of the hoof horn causing weak and brittle hoofs.

Confinement also diminishes the amount of internal moisture a hoof receives from blood flow. An idle horse has stagnant circulation,

127. *The yearling may have misshapen or badly chipped feet requiring shoes.*

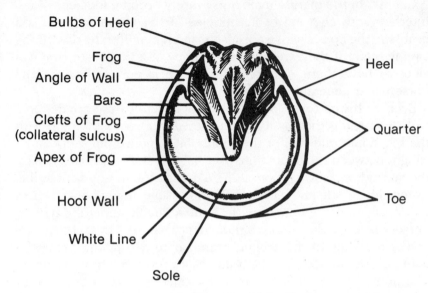

Bulbs of Heel

Frog

Angle of Wall

Bars

Clefts of Frog (collateral sulcus)

Apex of Frog

Hoof Wall

White Line

Sole

Heel

Quarter

Toe

The Parts of the Hoof

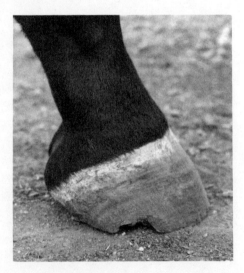

128. *This front foot chip, left unattended, may lead to weak quarters and heels.*

which results in fewer nutrients being delivered to the hoof, fewer waste products being removed, and less internal moisture being distributed.

You should keep your young horse's hooves clean and dry to prevent **thrush**. Watch for the development of weak heels and other hoof irregularities such as flares, club feet, or thin soles. Working closely with a veterinarian and farrier can minimize the effects of such problems.

Handling the foal's feet and legs before the first hoof-trimming will allow the farrier to do his best work and will reduce stress on both the foal and the farrier. A foal should have his feet checked at about one to two months of age and every month thereafter until he is a year old. Scheduling farrier care every six to eight weeks will ensure service before problems get out of hand. Some yearlings and two-year-olds may require shoeing to encourage balanced hoof growth, for protection, or for therapeutic reasons (photos 127–131).

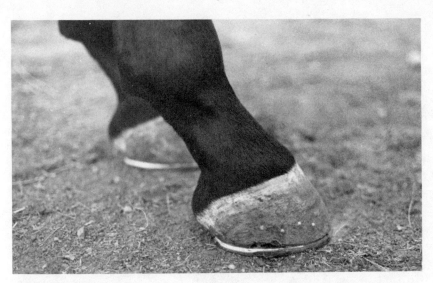

129. The protected chip.

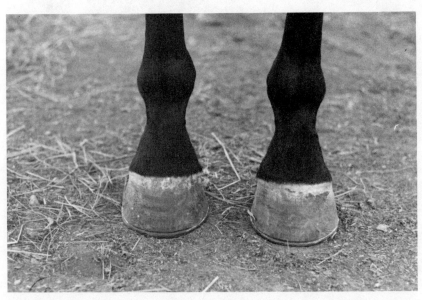

130. Shoes protect the hoofs and, if regularly reset, can maintain proper hoof balance.

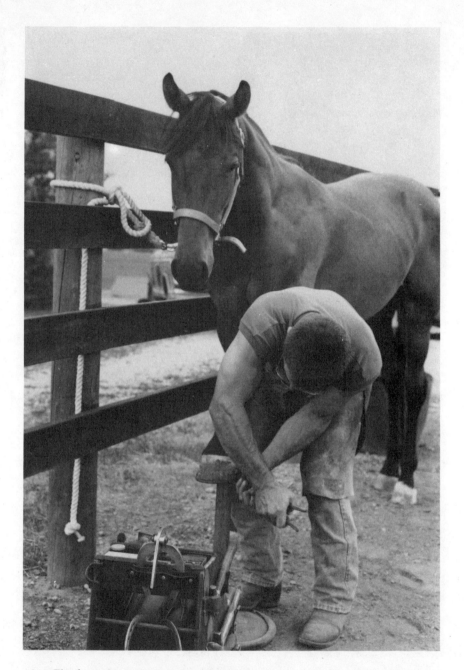

131. The first shoeing presents a few new lessons, but the horse with systematic training takes it right in stride.

MANE AND TAIL CARE

A healthy, flowing tail adds elegance to a horse's appearance. More importantly, from the horse's perspective, a long tail is an efficient fly chaser. Tails can be used as an overall indicator of health and management.

A variety of factors affect the appearance of the tail. The hair-producing cells that line each follicular bulb are thought to go through growing and resting phases. Individual horses demonstrate variable lengths of these phases and subsequently have differing potential for long tail hair.

Each hair shaft has a cortex covered by a scalelike covering called the cuticle. Depending on the uniformity and strength of the cuticle, hairs may be resilient or brittle. Brittle hairs break before their time to shed, so the tail never reaches its full potential.

Many management practices can affect the quality of the keratin-ized protein that makes up hair. An adequate quantity and quality of essential amino acids in the diet assures that your horse has the ingredients to produce good quality hoof horn and hair. If your horse's hair is dull or rough or his hooves are brittle and shelly, you should test his feed to determine if it provides adequate quantities of the essential amino acids methionine and tryptophan.

Feeding your horse two ounces of vegetable oil twice daily with his grain ration will provide additional unsaturated fatty acids that will make his coat shinier. After six to seven weeks of oil supplementation you should see a change.

Tail Rubbing

Horses who rub their tails usually do so initially for a specific reason; however, they may continue the habit long after the cause has been removed. Therefore, it is of utmost importance to locate the problem early. Possible causes include, but are not limited to, a dirty sheath or udder, parasites, fungus, or dandruff.

Male horses most often rub their tails because of a dirty sheath. Fatty secretions, dead skin cells, and dirt accumulate in the sheath area. This black, sticky substance, called smegma, may need to be removed as often as four times a year or as seldom as every two or three years, depending on the individual.

To clean the sheath you can either reach up into it or you can encourage the horse to "let down" (lower his penis). Scratching a gelding over the kidneys (loin area), especially when he is relaxed, such as after a workout, often makes him lower his penis. The first time you clean the sheath you can also tranquilize the horse to reduce stress and anxiety. If a very heavy accumulation of smegma is present, you may want to apply mineral oil, Vaseline petroleum jelly, or glycerin and leave it on for several days to loosen the debris. Oil will attract more dirt, however, so it is important to follow this pretreatment with several washings and adequate rinsing. If you follow a routine schedule of sheath cleaning, you should only need warm water and soap (photos 132–134).

Often a ball of smegma called a "bean" will accumulate in the diverticulum near the urethral opening (see illustration on facing page). This can build up to a size that could interfere with urination and should be removed when found.

132. When cleaning the sheath, the groom should maintain a safe position. With a well-lathered tube sock over her hand, she loosens the smegma.

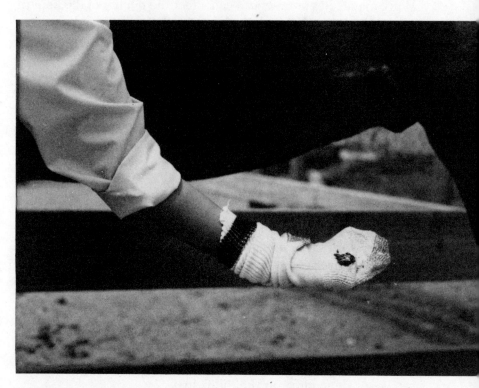

133. The black waxy exudate can be removed in large chunks.

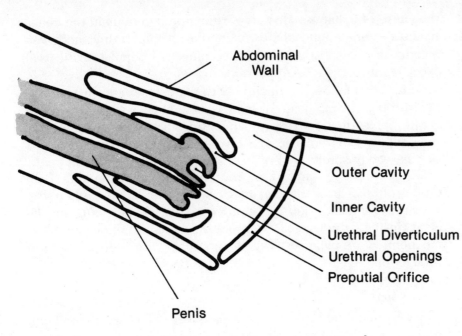

Abdominal Wall

Outer Cavity

Inner Cavity

Urethral Diverticulum

Urethral Openings

Preputial Orifice

Penis

The Anatomy of the Sheath

Mares produce a similar type of accumulation between the folds of the udder and may become tail-rubbers if this is neglected. Use the same procedures as for sheath cleaning. Remember to observe safety precautions whenever attempting to clean the sheath or udder of an animal that is unfamiliar with the process.

External parasites such as lice, mites, and ticks may drive a horse into an itching frenzy. Each must be diagnosed and treated separately. Lindane is an effective insecticide on all three insects mentioned and is often prescribed by veterinarians.

Pinworms, an internal parasite, can also be responsible for anal itch. They live in the large intestine, where they mate. The female then travels to the rectum where she protrudes her tail out of the anus and deposits egg clusters on the surrounding skin. The glue-like secretion that secures the egg to the anal mucosa appears to be

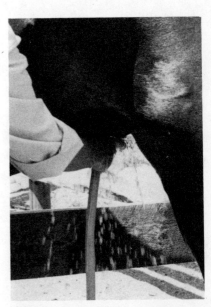

134. After washing the sheath with soap, rinse it thoroughly with warm water by inserting the hose into the sheath and flushing it with low water pressure.

the cause of irritation. Most deworming preparations in the benzimadazole, organophosphate, phenothiazine-piperazine, and ivermectin classes substantially reduce pinworm populations if used every eight weeks (see Appendix).

Fungus can follow the midline of the horse and appear from the poll through the tail head. Weladol is an iodine-based shampoo that is often prescribed to treat the area. Ringworm, a fungus infection, may appear as circular lesions anywhere on the body. This infection is readily spread by brushes, blankets, and girths.

The presence of dandruff on the **dock** may cause itching. Dandruff is often characteristic of an overweight, underexercised horse. It can also indicate skin irritation caused by overwashing, insufficient rinsing, or nonspecific dermatitis. Dry skin is often caused by biochemical imbalances which interfere with normal **sebum** production.

Tail Care

The tail should be inspected on a daily basis. To keep the tail long and full, gently untangle the hairs with your hands; this results in the least damage. After untangling the tail hairs, brush them lightly with a natural-bristle hair brush for humans. Using a plastic brush, plastic comb, or metal comb will cause more hair breakage.

The tail should be shampooed monthly if possible. This schedule usually keeps dirt to a minimum while not subjecting the skin to unnecessary irritation. It is best to use mild soaps, and to apply them primarily on the skin of the dock. Soap residues can cause tail rubbing, so be generous with rinse water.

If your horse's dock is too dry, a good mixture to use is ten to twenty parts baby oil to one part Absorbine liniment. The liniment is stimulating, cooling, and mildly antiseptic, while the baby oil is absorbed easily by the skin. The mixture should be applied at the roots of the hair, and after treatment the tail can be wrapped with a cotton bandage for several hours. If your horse has very sensitive skin, start with an even more diluted mixture or use plain baby oil.

If the skirt of your horse's tail is too dry, the best remedy is to apply a good quality hair conditioner to freshly shampooed hair while it is still wet. Then tie your horse in a shady area and do not comb or brush his tail until it is dry.

Tail Protection

Long tails can be protected in the months other than fly season by a combination of loose braiding and wrapping. The following method is quick and easy. First cut a ten-foot piece of gauze. Then, starting at the end of your horse's dock, divide his tail hair into three sections. Put the midpoint of the gauze behind the middle section and braid the tail with a conventional, three-strand braid, holding a piece of gauze with each of the outer sections while braiding. When you get to the end of the tail, you should have ample gauze left over to loop the braided tail through itself several times. Secure the loop closed with criss-cross or solid wraps. If this is done with moderate but even tension, the tail can be left braided for several weeks at a time with no harm.

If your horse has developed the habit of rubbing his tail you can install a hot wire from an electric fence on the perimeter of his stall or paddock to discourage him. If an electric wire is impractical, you can affix a tail board on its edge around the entire stall wall at a height to meet the buttocks at a point just below the dock. Cleanliness and good parasite-management practices are the biggest factors in maintaining a healthy tail.

Mane Care

Mane care has much in common with tail care. Sometimes, however, you may want to thin the mane and shorten it. This can be done several ways, but the best results are obtained by pulling the mane. To do this, wrap several of the longest underhairs around a pulling comb and then pull them from the mane. Plan to pull the mane over several sessions; this results in less irritation to the horse than if it is all done on one afternoon. You can also numb the root area, or crest of the mane, with a little liniment to make the experience possibly more pleasant for your horse.

When you are braiding manes and tails, always use thread or yarn instead of rubber bands to minimize hair breakage, and remove tight braids as soon as possible.

TWELVE

Nutrition

THE DIGESTIVE SYSTEM

The modern horse has evolved from browsers and grazers who ate many small meals of brush and dried grasses. The adult equine digestive system is designed to handle a continuous supply of roughages in its cecum. This blind pouch off the large intestine is where high-fiber feeds are broken down into more usable constituents.

The foal has a simple type of digestive system with most of the processes occurring in the stomach and small intestine. The large intestine and cecum become more involved with digestion by the time the foal is six months old. This change corresponds to the transition in the foal's diet from milk to hay. In the first three months of life, a foal can suffer from diarrhea if he eats foods too high in fiber, so it is imperative to offer only high-quality leafy hay.

NUTRIENTS

The six nutrient groups are: water, carbohydrates, fats, protein, minerals, and vitamins.

Water

Horses drink one half to one gallon of water per 100 pounds of body weight daily for maintenance. The need for water will be affected by environmental temperature, level of exercise, and type of feed ration. Always provide good, quality, free-choice water. Horses do not necessarily drink when it is convenient for their owners, but rather as part of their daily routine. Insufficient water can depress appetite and lead to **impaction** colic.

Carbohydrates

There are three sources of energy: carbohydrates, fats, and proteins. A horse's energy requirements depend on his weight, activity level, and stage of lactation. Always feed by weight, not volume. A one-pound coffee can holds approximately one pound of oats or one-half pound of bran or one and one-half pounds of corn or pelleted feeds. You should actually weigh the filled can or container to ascertain the exact amount being fed (photo 135).

Carbohydrates in horse feeds are usually in the form of sugars, starches, and cellulose, with the cellulose predominantly fiber. Most of the energy value of a feed comes from its sugar and starch content.

Fats

Fats are a concentrated source of energy, providing 2.25 times as much energy as an equal weight of carbohydrates or proteins. The horse can tolerate up to 16 percent fat in his total ration. Typically, the horse diet contains 2 to 6 percent fat.

Protein

Although protein is not economical to feed specifically for its energy content, the horse's body can utilize excess protein for energy. Be careful though. Feeding high levels of protein can be harmful. Excess protein in the diet causes the liver and kidneys to work overtime and increases the horse's need for water to flush waste products from the body. Excess protein can also contribute to bone problems in growing horses.

Protein is made up of various combinations of the twenty-two amino acids. Some of these amino acids can be synthesized in the horse's body, while others—called essential amino acids—must be supplied every day in his feed ration. Feeds high in essential amino acids are said to have high-quality protein. The three amino acids that are most limited in horse rations are lysine, methionine, and tryptophan. Lysine especially is important for growth. Since feeds vary in the quality of protein they contain, you may need to supplement your young horse's ration with lysine. Ask your veterinarian for his or her opinion.

135. Feed by weight not by volume. This "three pound" coffee can when full really holds from one and a half to four pounds of grain. Feeds vary greatly and each must be weighed separately.

If a horse is fed more protein than he needs, his body removes the nitrogen, in the form of ammonia, from the protein and uses the balance for energy. If energy is not needed, the balance is stored as fat. The ammonia that is removed accounts for the characteristic strong smell in the urine of horses on high-protein diets.

Minerals

The amount and balance of minerals are important for many bodily functions. Horses should always have free-choice trace-mineral salt, which provides sodium, chloride, and other **electrolytes**. In addition, you should be very conscious of the amount and ratio of calcium and phosphorus in a young horse's diet.

It is best to keep the calcium:phosphorus ratio in the ration of the growing horse between 2:1 and 1:1. You should analyze hay to determine its actual nutrient composition and carefully examine any supplements you feed your horse to determine their contribution to the overall calcium:phosphorus balance.

Calcium deficiencies can cause the body to mobilize calcium from the bones, which then weakens the skeletal structure. Excess phosphorus can create a calcium deficiency that is commonly displayed in leg problems such as enlarged joints or epiphysitis.

Copper and zinc are also essential elements for the young, growing horse.

Vitamins

Most vitamins are present in adequate quantities in a horse's ration. Vitamin A would be the only vitamin that you may want to supplement if your horse is fed a steady diet of old, bleached forages. The liver, however, can store a six-month supply of vitamin A. Oversupplementation usually creates more of a problem with horses than do dietary deficiencies.

FEEDS

The mare's milk provides all the necessary nutrients for the foal until he is about three months old. However, within the first one to two weeks, the foal should begin consuming solid feed as an additional source of nutrition.

Roughages are fed to the horse in the form of hay or pasture, with hays generally **legume**, grass, or cereal grain hay. The major legumes fed to horses are alfalfa and clover. Grasses include but are not limited to timothy, brome, and orchard grass. Oat hay, in which the grain has not been harvested, can also make suitable horse forage.

Alfalfa is higher in nutritional value than an equal amount of quality grass hay, having at least twice as much protein, three times the amount of calcium, and many more vitamins. If good quality alfalfa is available in your area, it is highly recommended for the growing horse.

Hay quality is determined by the stage of maturity during which the field was cut, the growing conditions, the field management, and the weather during the curing and baling process. Good hay is free of mold, dust, and weeds and has a bright green color and a fresh smell. The leaf-to-stem ratio is high and the hay is soft to the touch, with little shattering of leaves but no excess moisture that could cause overheating and spoilage. Since hay comprises the mainstay of the horse's ration, you should locate the very best hay available for your growing horse.

Pasture provides necessary exercise and nutrients for the young horse. One acre of improved pasture with adequate moisture or irrigation can support two horses during a six-month grazing season. However, you may need fifty or more acres of dry rangeland to support a single horse. Local extension agents can assist you in choosing the best plant varieties and management procedures for your situation.

Concentrates are feeds that are low in fiber but high in energy, such as grains and protein supplements. Oats have become a traditional horse feed because of the safe ratio of fiber to energy that their hulls provide. A highly digestible grain such as corn, with its thin seed coat, has the potential of being too concentrated for the horse's diet. On an energy basis, oats are about the most expensive grain, while corn is an economic source of concentrated energy. There are a lot of old wives' tales circulating about corn: that it is a "hot" feed, that it will make horses fat or too spirited, and that it causes founder. The truth is that because of its density, corn has twice the energy value of an equal volume of oats. So if you feed corn by the coffee-can method (volume instead of weight), your horses *can* suffer these feared consequences because they are getting twice what they should (see photo 135).

Feeding extra corn in cold weather can actually be counterproductive. Horses gain body heat from the heat of digestion. Since corn is relatively quickly digested, it offers little body heat. Hay, on the other hand, requires a longer digestion time and subsequently warms the body. Feeding corn prior to the cold season to fatten and insulate a horse has some basis in fact but is not recommended for young horses. Feeding a balanced, high-quality ration year-round is preferred.

At the head of the protein supplement list is soybean meal, which contains the highest quality protein and the highest amount of lysine of any plant source. It is the supplement of choice in rations for growing horses.

Commercially prepared horse feeds are available as pellets or grain mixes. Pelleted feeds may be forages, concentrates, or a combination of forages and concentrates. "Sweet feed" grain mixes are usually a combination of oats and/or barley, corn, molasses, and a pellet comprised of soybean meal, minerals, and vitamins. Feed mills create different products to correspond to the needs of the various classes of horses and usually have several feeds to choose from for the growing horse (see Appendix for ration guidelines).

FEEDING RECOMMENDATIONS FOR YOUNG HORSES

A laboratory analysis of hay and grain is the simplest, best, and most direct method to determine exactly what a horse is being fed. Your veterinarian or nutritionist can advise you on sampling procedures and can assist in interpreting results and making supplement corrections.

With a young horse it is best to feed at least twice and preferably three times a day and at the same time every day. His feed areas should be free from fecal contamination (photo 136). Choose safe feeders that do not encourage chewing on facilities (photos 137 and 138), and feed forages at ground level whenever possible. Group forage feeding is acceptable as long as there is enough feed for the level of competition in the group.

136. *Feeding forages on the ground constitutes a natural state for horses.
Be sure the area is free from manure and subsequent parasite
contamination.*

137. A pasture grain feeder can be made from two tires and a rubber bucket.

Always feed by weight, not volume. From birth to two years of age, the horse should have access to free-choice trace-mineralized salt, water, and high-quality forage. Determine your horse's needs for added concentrates and mineral supplements by analyzing his hay and then referring to requirement charts. Be sure to always monitor your young horse's calcium:phosphorus ratio closely (photo 139).

Make all increases and decreases of concentrates gradually: Change by half-pound increments and hold for four feedings before making another adjustment. All changes from one type of forage to another should similarly take place over a period of time. For optimum results, feed each young horse his concentrate ration separately.

Be sure your young horse has had a "full feed" of hay before turning him out on pasture for the first time; otherwise he may eat too much grass and founder. Initially, limit the amount of time he spends on pasture to a half hour and gradually increase it.

Be conservative about offering creep feed to nursing foals. By two months of age, the foal will be nibbling out of the dam's feed box. Begin offering your foal small amounts of high-quality food in a **creep feeder** when he is about three months old. Feed measured amounts, avoiding the free-choice, full-volume creep feeder. Be sure the feed is fresh each day.

Discourage vices such as wood chewing by providing adequate roughage and exercise.

138. *A feeder like this is safe and indestructible.*

139. *Mineral and protein blocks can provide entertainment as well as nourishment. Be sure you have selected the proper block for your feeding situation.*

THIRTEEN

Confinement and Exercise

If your young horse lives in other than a pasture situation, you must take care when designing his facilities. Keeping a weanling or yearling in a separate stall or pen at feeding time is a good way to ensure that he is getting a specific ration. A 10 × 10-foot box stall is adequate for young stock of most breeds, but it is unreasonable to expect an energetic foal to spend more than 50 percent of his time confined.

Solid walls make the safest stalls and board or pipe fencing works well for pens or small paddocks. Be sure all gates are secure and made of safe materials. Wood and tubular-metal gates are greatly preferred over wire and sheet-metal gates. Some metal gates unmercifully peel the hide off a horse's leg if it is caught between the slats. Choose your fencing carefully. Do not use barbed wire unless absolutely necessary; barbed wire and young horses make a volatile mixture. Enough accidents happen in seemingly safe facilities—there is no sense inviting trouble with old, worn materials, crowded pens, or poor design.

Exercise is essential for the proper development of a young horse (photo 140). Suckling and weanling foals are characteristically insecure, vulnerable, excitable, and unpredictable. Providing a safe and healthy outlet for their energy is a challenge to the most accomplished of horsemen.

A regular conditioning program invigorates the foal's appetite, tones his muscles, increases his lung and heart capacities, and helps him develop reflexes and coordination. Vigorous playing over varied terrain toughens his hooves, tendons, and bones; and regular stress creates dense, stress-resistant bone. Allowing young horses to play in moderately soft footing can help develop elasticity in their tendons. Lack of exercise, on the other hand, can cause contracted flexor tendons.

174

140. *Free exercise for the foal and dam.*

Horses who are allowed ample exercise rarely develop vices such as pawing, stall kicking, or wood chewing, which are often the results of boredom. In addition, regularly exercised foals are less prone to uncontrollable bursts of exuberance that can lead to injury (photo 141). To be most effective, exercise should be a regular part of your young horse's daily routine. Planned exercise should involve gradual increases, starting with a proper warmup before strenuous activity and ending with a cool-down.

Foals can become overfatigued easily. Just a few minutes of excess exertion can lead to long-term bone and soft-tissue disorders. Footing should be soft, but not excessively deep for the foal, as hyperextension of the fetlock in deep sand can permanently weaken tendons. Since a foal's vision is not very sharp for the first week after birth, it is important that you turn the youngster out in a safely fenced area, free from hazardous objects. Many foals are quite timid when introduced to horses other than their own dams, so it is best to socialize them gradually.

Whenever you implement a regimented conditioning program be sure to carefully monitor signs of stress to prevent serious injury. Be sure your foal is not overweight. Overweight foals have a much greater potential for injury during exercise than do foals of healthy weight. Check the croup, withers, and neck for excess fat. Consult with your veterinarian regarding your foal's diet.

The best exercise choice for the suckling foal is free exercise with his dam. The second day after the foal's birth you can turn him out with his dam for about fifteen minutes, and by the time the foal is two weeks old you can increase his exercise to free choice providing he has privacy and shelter for proper resting. For the first several weeks, the foal is usually content to gallop increasingly larger circles around his dam. By four weeks, most foals seek the

141. A confined yearling pulls dangerous stunts at exercise time.

companionship of other foals for gymnastic play, and by eight weeks, foals spend over 50 percent of their waking hours away from their dam. Socialization with other mares and their foals is important for the foal. He will learn acceptable limits of behavior while at the same time developing his competitive spirit.

Perhaps the simplest and safest way to begin an organized workout for the foal is to pony his dam from another horse and let the foal follow. It is best not to ride the nursing mare or work her too hard when she is lactating heavily. Limit the exercise to walking in an enclosed area, and use a very well-behaved pony horse. Formal exercise for the youngster doesn't usually begin until the yearling year.

In-hand lessons are a labor-intensive way of providing exercise for your horses (photo 141). However, there are advantages. The fractious outbursts characteristic in free exercise are minimized because of the close control. In addition, the young horse is being trained. In-hand sessions with suckling foals are generally limited to work at the walk and trot and backing (see Chapter 4).

After weaning and into the yearling year, your foal can begin a formal exercise program if necessary. Free exercise (photo 142) and ponying are still the best choices. Ponying the young horse on the surface on which he will be worked when he is an adult provides him with an opportunity for specialized adaptation of tissues. A variety in scenery and experiences also strengthens his mental development.

Longeing is another popular form of exercise you can incorporate into your program (see Part Two, Chapter 7).

Using an electric horse walker for occasional sessions with a young horse can be useful. If you are too busy to work your horse, walking him thirty minutes once or twice a week with the horse walker can be a good alternative. Depending entirely on a walker for exercise, however, is not good, as the walker encourages the young horse to develop a stiff carriage and become resistant, lazy, and bored. Horses that have had successful lessons in leading and tying adapt to work on the walker easily.

Treadmills can similarly be used for an occasional workout, providing the young horse is gradually conditioned to the work and carefully monitored for signs of stress. A continuous climb at the five- to seven-degree slope characteristic of most treadmills is extremely fatiguing. Getting the young horse to enter the treadmill

142. Horses will follow their natural instincts in spite of domestication pressures.

the first time may be difficult unless he has had similar lessons, such as loading in a two-horse trailer.

When you use a treadmill, you horse's workout will be accomplished in about half the time required for most other forms of exercise. Be careful not to overuse the treadmill. If you ask your young horse to perform on it for just a few minutes beyond his physical capabilities, he may develop a sullen attitude toward future work. Treadmills can be successfully used to condition halter horses when muscle development is desired, particularly in the forearm, chest, stifle, and gaskin areas.

Occasional swimming is another good form of exercise for the young horse. Swimming minimizes trauma to the joints while maximizing muscle development and condition.

FOURTEEN

Stress

Stress is a demand for adaptation. In the wild, horses have the choice to flee rather than confront their fears. Domestication requires horses to learn to live in the human's world. Each horse has his own **stress tolerance level**. When domestication pressures and demands exceed a horse's capacity to adapt, he will fail. This failure can be seen in the forms of behavior abnormalities (vices or bad habits), illness, or injury.

Stress is essential for the mental and physical development of an individual. Although some situations require intense confrontation, gradual exposure to stress is often appropriate. The goal of interval training, for example, is gradual adaptation to stress. Interval training achieves these goals by alternating stimulating episodes with rest or nonstressful activities, with the stimulation gradually increased.

Parameters that can be altered to change a horse's stress threshold are the frequency of the stress, the intensity of the stress, the speed of onset, and the duration of the stress. If you are using a canter for conditioning purposes, for example, you can vary the number of times you canter your horse during a training session, the speed of each canter, the length of the precanter warmup, the activity immediately preceding the canter (breaking from a standstill versus cantering from a trot), and the length of time you ask your horse to canter.

Similarly, habituation is a way of gradually exposing a horse to psychological pressures. If you eventually want to be able to take off your jacket while you are mounted, you begin by allowing the horse to inspect and accept the sight and smell of a soft jacket. Over several sessions, you gradually increase how suddenly you present the jacket to the horse, how fast you flap it, how intensely you flap

179

it, and for how long you flap it. You can also vary the intensity of the stimulus by substituting a noisy raincoat for the soft jacket.

Sometimes it is necessary to confront a horse with his fears. Lessons such as tying and picking up the feet are in this category. You can't gradually tie a horse or partially pick up his feet; these are some of the "all or none" situations in horse training. If you plan your session carefully, using proper principles, facilities, and equipment, a confrontation can become a positive addition to the horse's experience. During a confrontation, a horse learns clearly what works and what doesn't. Horses are insecure followers who do not know the difference between "good" and "bad." They form habits in accordance with their experiences. In the majority of confrontation training sessions, the horse will learn the lesson if you make your wants clear.

In some cases, where the basics have not been firmly established, a horse can become uncooperative and sullen when confronted. A sullen horse characteristically "tunes out" the lesson by holding his breath, biting his tongue, holding eyes at half mast, and/or leaning into heavy pressure. A sharp noise or slap of your hand should get your horse's attention back. Be careful, though; his reaction may be explosive as he instinctively sucks in air to fill the oxygen debt.

Most horses indicate they are suffering from extreme stress by showing either anxiety or depression. Today's horses experience four main types of stress: psychological, immunological, metabolic, and mechanical. The cause for most psychological stress lies in the horse's innate desire to flee from danger and seek the security of his herdmates. You will gradually diminish your horse's flight reflex and develop an independent attitude in him in his early training lessons.

When you restrain a foal with your arms until he relaxes, this is the first reassurance to him that flight is not necessary nor desired in your world. Letting the foal go after he has quit struggling is a reinforcement of the desired behavior. Older horses who have not learned this necessary submission/relaxation lesson may constantly test your dominance. Horses are much more secure and cooperative when the rules are made clear.

Weaning has the potential for causing the foal great psychological distress (photo 143). You should minimize physical stress at weaning by making sure the foal is eating at least five pounds of

143. Psychological Stress: This weanling misses his dam's companionship more than her milk.

high-quality hay per day plus an appropriate amount of creep feed. The mare's milk production declines drastically when the foal is four months old, so the foal's system is not affected much by that dietary change. Make sure immunizations, deworming, and hoof care are current at weaning time so no potentially stressful situation is scheduled for the week or so following the foal's separation from his dam.

Most weaning methods are based on minimizing either the duration of the foal's anxiety or the intensity of it. Abrupt weaning, with mare and foal out of sight and sound of each other, may be intense at first, but the trauma is short in duration. Gradual weaning may spread the distress out over several weeks, but because separation

144. *Psychological Stress: An insecure or lonely horse may find comfort in a stable companion.*

is for short periods of time and often with the dam and foal near each other, the intensity of the foal's concern is minimized.

Whatever weaning method you chose, you should leave the foal in his familiar environment and remove the mare to safe facilities. Never underestimate the potential frenzy of a newly weaned foal. Be sure fences are safe and strong and there are no dangerous objects in the foal's environment. If you have handled the foal independently while he was still a suckling, he is more likely to go through weaning without a sound. Providing him with a companion foal will help alleviate his loneliness.

It is important to note that young horses must not only be weaned from their dams, but eventually also from their herdmates. Turning several weanlings out together only transfers the bond from mother to playmate, and you may encounter a similar dependency when you try to handle the youngsters separately. Therefore, it is wise to treat the young horse as a separate entity from birth onward. Scheduling periodic halter lessons, feeding foals separately, and introducing them to varied combinations of older horses as soon as it is practical will encourage independence. While occasionally you may need to provide a companion animal for a lonely horse (photo 144), you should watch for signs of overdependency.

Although a trailer ride can provide some psychological concerns for a horse, it also introduces many physical stresses. The fatigue that horses experience from a long trip is caused primarily by an unstable environment. Before shipping, evaluate the temperature, air flow, humidity, space, noise, footing, air pressure (hauling at high altitudes or flying), and the direction the horse is facing in relation to the direction of travel. Often a small adjustment will dissipate a horse's uneasiness. You can help relieve stress with such small touches as putting cotton in his ears, securing a rattling stall divider, spreading sawdust on the floor, and adjusting an overhead vent.

Horses are often blanketed too heavily when traveling. Overheating can lead to lethargy and depression, and if an animal sweats and is then chilled, he may get muscle spasms. Skeletal muscles can cramp and digestive muscles can become hypermotile, which leads to dehydration.

Horses are subjected to immunological stress from both their natural environment and vaccinations (photo 145). Immunization schedules are designed to gradually and repeatedly stress the immune system to develop a strong defense against various diseases. About a year after most injections, the antibody titers drop, weakening the horse's defense. Therefore, you will need to restimulate or restress your horse's immune system periodically to boost the potential antibody protection.

Some vaccines must be given once a year for optimum protection. However, you will need to give more frequent boosters for the respiratory diseases (influenza and rhinopneumonitis) to horses in high-risk situations.

Metabolic stresses are dangerous conditions that affect fit, well-cared-for athletes as well as overweight or malnourished horses. A common underlying cause of many of these conditions is an electrolyte imbalance. The initial cause may be overexertion, severe injury, illness, or body upsets that result in a horse going off his feed or water (photo 146). When a horse loses a great amount of important

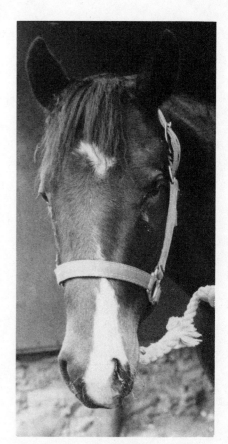

145. Immunological Stress: Young horses are particularly susceptible to respiratory infections.

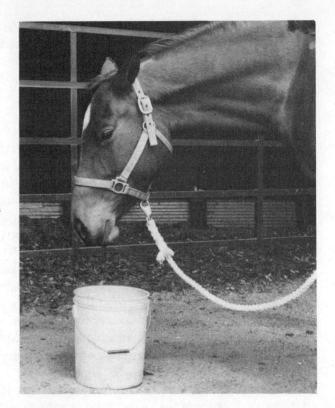

146. Metabolic Stress: You can lead a horse to water, but you can't make him drink.

body fluids (water or blood) and fails to replenish them, an electrolyte deficit or imbalance results.

When tissue ion concentrations are low or imbalanced in sodium, potassium, calcium, or chloride, muscles can become weak or spasm. The horse's desire to drink or eat is diminished, further compounding the effects of dehydration.

Foals who are dehydrated can become apathetic and lose their sucking reflex. Dosing a dehydrated horse with an electrolyte solution will give him the necessary energy and interest for recovery. Since a horse's body chemistry operates on a delicate balance, you should get your veterinarian's advice before giving electrolytes to your horse.

There is a fine line between a conditioning effect and mechanical stress. Although horses need a certain amount of bone concussion, muscle fatigue, and tendon stretching to achieve a useful athletic condition, conditioning can be overdone and early signs of stress are often undetected (photo 147).

Working a horse on hard ground may be exactly what he needs to develop tough hoofs, durable ligaments, and dense bone columns for eventing or endurance riding, yet it can also become his downfall if in the process he acquires sole bruises or arthritis.

The surface of the terrain on which you work a horse can create enormous differences in his stress levels. The hardness, depth of footing, incline, and irregularity of the surface all have the potential to strengthen or weaken an individual. Intense conditioning programs are not usually designed for horses under two years of age unless the horses are being prepared for racing.

Bone growth and nourishment take place in several areas in the horse: the marrow cavity, the epiphyseal (physeal) plates in young horses, and the periosteum. The latter, the thin, tough bone-skin with a large blood and nerve supply, is the site where ligaments and tendons attach to bones and is responsible for increasing the diameter of the shaft of long bones (see illustration on page 186).

The length of the long bones is increased at the growth plates at each end of the bone shaft. Every cartilaginous zone of bone proliferation (area of bone growth) has its own predetermined time of closure (see "Ranges of Growth Plate Closure" in Appendix).

Joints vary in design and type of movement, but all have thick,

147. *Mechanical Stress: Hyperextension of the fetlock can cause tendon and/or bone damage.*

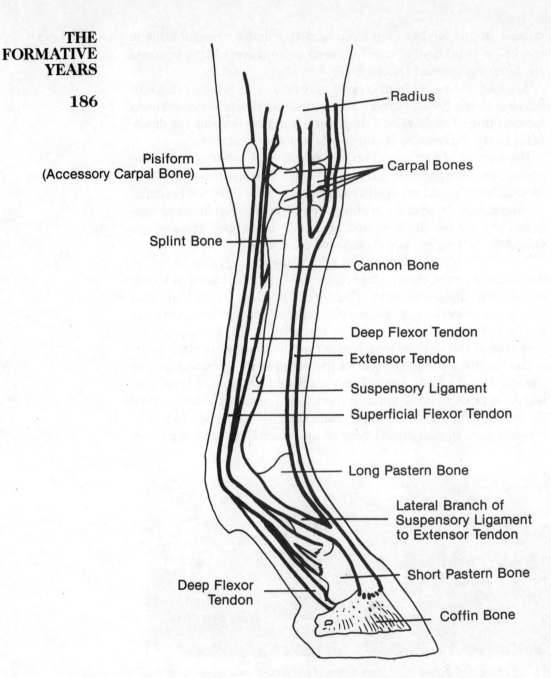

Radius

Pisiform
(Accessory Carpal Bone)

Carpal Bones

Splint Bone

Cannon Bone

Deep Flexor Tendon

Extensor Tendon

Suspensory Ligament

Superficial Flexor Tendon

Long Pastern Bone

Lateral Branch of
Suspensory Ligament
to Extensor Tendon

Short Pastern Bone

Deep Flexor
Tendon

Coffin Bone

The Major Tendons and Bones of the Front Leg

smooth cartilage covering the articulating surfaces for protection and durability. Encased in a capsule with a secretory membrane, joints receive lubrication from synovial fluid.

The front leg is a column of bones that provides the framework for the structures responsible for movement, support, and shock absorption. At rest, the front legs bear 65 to 72 percent of the horse's body weight plus part of the weight of the rider and tack. At a canter or gallop, the leading foreleg can bear as much as 3000 pounds. A horse with downhill conformation or one who travels heavy on the forehand undergoes an even greater loading. It is no wonder that 80 percent of lamenesses involve the front legs.

Joints experience two kinds of stress. As the horse's leg strikes the ground and bears weight, the articular surfaces are subjected to concussion. Abnormally upright bone alignment can contribute to damage from concussive forces (photo 148).

As the leg bearing the horse's weight begins to push the horse forward and upward, the bones and associated structures are compressed. It is in this phase that stretching and tearing of ligaments and tendons and chipping of bones can occur. Long, sloping pasterns or hooves with a long toe and low heel can intensify the forces of compression, particularly in the navicular area. Correctly conformed pasterns and hooves provide the horse with necessary shock absorption without undue stress (photo 149).

Most joints of the front leg demonstrate only anterior-posterior movement, that is, frontward and backward motion of flexion and extension. The coffin joint, in addition, exhibits some mediolateral (side to side) movement.

The horse's knee is comprised of two rows of short bones that are attached to each other and to the radius and cannon bones by many ligaments. The accessory carpal bone (pisiform) lies behind the knee, and the flexor tendons utilize the pisiform's notched inner surface as a guide and brace. The pisiform supports tendons during movement and allows them to work at a better mechanical advantage by acting as a fulcrum for their pull.

The cannon is actually a round bone in spite of its frequent assessment for flatness. "Flat," in this instance, actually refers to tight, well-defined flexor tendons that stand out behind the cannon in a clean, sharp line. This "flatness" is desirable because it indicates that the tendons have room to move most efficiently.

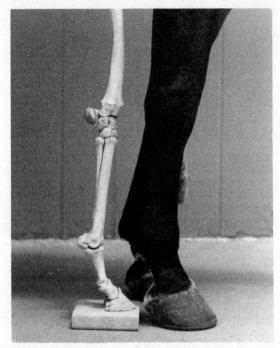

148. *A pastern that is more upright than desired.*

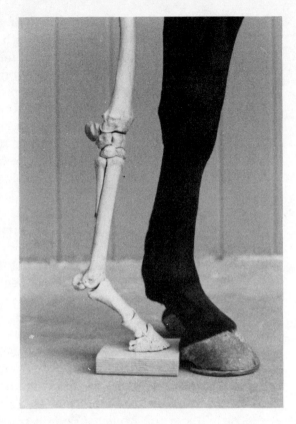

149. *A desirable sloping pastern.*

The upper ends of the splint bones help to form the base of the knee joint while the lower ends taper to a point. In young horses, the splint bones are attached to the cannon by interosseous ligaments, which, when inflamed, can lead to **splints**. The alley on the back of the cannon that is formed by the two splint bones provides a secure place for the upper portion of the suspensory ligaments to lie.

The lower portion of the cannon bone and the upper long pastern bone (first phalanx or P1) meet at the fetlock joint. The ridge on the cannon's joint surface and the groove on P1 ensure that the fetlock acts as a true hinge joint with flexion and extension only. Flexion in this instance is when the horse's leg is up and back, extension when the weight of the horse is pushing the fetlock down, and hyperextension when the fetlock approaches or touches the earth.

Assisting the fetlock joint in its stress-absorbing role are the **proximal** sesamoids. These triangular bones position the tendons at a more advantageous angle for flexion. They serve as a pulley and guide for the flexor tendons, which run between and over the sesamoids. In addition, the sesamoids provide a point of anchoring for the suspensory branches as they wrap around to their junction with the extensor tendon. When the horse turns, pressure on the fetlock is greatest where the tendons stretch and pull sideways, causing uneven strain on the joint.

The horse's leg below the fetlock corresponds to the human finger. The junction of P1 and P2 (second phalanx or short pastern bone) is known as the pastern. In a normal stance, the pastern should be parallel with the front edge of the coffin bone or the front of the hoof wall in a normally configured foot. At rest the front pastern and hoof-wall angle of most horses is 54 to 59 degrees; the hind angle is 55 to 60 degrees. At the trot the pastern angle decreases to 40 degrees and at the gallop to 20 degrees or less.

The coffin joint (P2 and P3) exhibits a considerable range of motion despite its encasement in the rigid hoof structure. The coffin bone of the front leg is much rounder than that of the hind, encouraging **breakover** at the toe. The pointed hind coffin allows mediolateral breakover necessary for hindquarter propulsion and direction initiation and change.

The navicular bone lies between the wings of the coffin bone and acts as a support and brace for the deep flexor tendon as it makes its way to its attachment on the bottom of the coffin bone. The navicular bone's ridge and the deep flexor tendon's corresponding groove stabilize the pulley system.

The navicular bone can experience great pressure depending on the individual horse's conformation, activity, and hoof balance or shoeing. The long-toe, low-heel syndrome makes the deep flexor tendon put added pressure on the navicular bursa. Caulks, stickers, and grabs on the horse's shoes inhibit the turning of the hoof on the ground surface in response to pressures tending to rotate the hoof. This strain often intensifies internally at the navicular bone.

Joints are said to be clean when the soft tissue structures surrounding the bone are tight and there is no excess swelling or fluid. A stressed and stretched joint capsule will appear distended at the points of stress and will be likely to carry extra fluid even after the cause for inflammation has been removed.

It is desirable for the horse's knee, hock, and fetlocks to be big (roomy, not meaty) in relation to the cannon to encourage freedom of movement, to provide adequate shock absorption because of greater articulating surface area, and to allow ample room for attachment and passage of the necessary tendons and ligaments.

The substance of bone is often indicated by the size of the cannon bone. More important than the actual circumference of the bone is its proportion to the horse's mature body size.

Various bones combine different proportions of resilience and strength to perform specified tasks. Collagen, a fibrous protein also found in tendons and ligaments, contributes to bone elasticity, which is necessary when the horse hyperextends at the gallop, for example. As the horse's weight descends, the flexor tendons pull upward; the knee is relatively unyielding. The give or bend, especially in the softer cannons of the young horse, safeguards against fractures.

Strength of bone comes from the density of minerals, particularly calcium, that fill the bone's collagenous latticework. Overfeeding young horses for early growth can result in a large but porous and weak frame caused by too much bone being added too quickly.

It is essential that your horse's hooves are properly balanced and shaped to ensure that his bone columns receive well-distributed weight. Closely monitored, regular stress is necessary for adequate bone development without breakdown.

Bone is capable of adaptive remodeling. This is the ability of tissues to adjust to new requirements of a specific physical activity or condition. Depending on the particular activity and mineral stores available, calcification will take place in areas of stress. Asymmetric limbs, for example, commonly develop added bone at the splints and at the hock, fetlock, and pastern joints. During the period of active bone remodeling, the horse may be sore or lame for several weeks, yet once the calcification has taken place the horse often returns to work with little, if any, pain and varying losses in range of motion.

Horses are dealt a genetic alignment formula from their parents. This inherited structure can be affected prior to birth by their uterine position or by the nutrition of the dam. The skeletal conformation can be further altered by nutritional strategies in the first two years of life.

FIFTEEN

Puberty

During his yearling and two-year-old years, the young horse is making the transition from childhood into young adulthood. It is a time of moodiness, periodic silliness, and testiness intermingled with some very adult behavior. This unpredictability makes this an appropriate time to let the youngsters grow up and "be horses."

GELDING AND AFTERCARE

Castration is a common procedure for 90 percent of domestic male horses. Only the very best individuals should be kept for breeding purposes; the rest should be castrated or gelded. Geldings generally have a more stable disposition than either stallions or mares and are suitable for a wide range of uses.

Male hormones are responsible for much more than the desire and capability to breed mares. Athletic performance can be helped or hindered by testosterone. Many stallions perform with more gusto than a gelding. However, one of the undesirable secondary sex characteristics that can result from testosterone production in the stallion may be overdeveloped muscles. A cresty or thick neck, for example, can decrease flexibility and handiness.

The ungelded yearling will often display stallion mannerisms such as loud whinnying, fractious behavior, and sexual interest in mares. Although gelding will not change unwanted manners, it will eventually remove the tendencies toward them.

When to geld is largely a management decision. Often facilities require a compatible mixing of the sexes, so many people geld a horse at twelve months. However, it is best to assess each individual

191

to determine the optimum gelding time. Some eight-month-old weanlings mount fences in an attempt to get at mares in heat, squeal, strike, and begin developing a thick neck. Others only quietly watch the mares and keep a streamlined conformation until well into their two-year-old year.

Early spring is a preferred season for gelding because flies are not yet a serious problem and the heat of the day will not contribute to swelling. Late fall is equally popular for the same reasons. Avoid gelding in very cold weather since in the cold the colt is less likely to exercise sufficiently to avoid preputial edema (swelling).

Proper health-management practices contribute to safe and easy recovery from this minor surgery. Check with your veterinarian to be sure your horse's vaccination and deworming is current before you schedule an appointment for gelding. Parasites can steal nutrients necessary for your horse's healing process. Tetanus protection is especially important when dealing with a wound or incision.

Look at your facilities and find a clean, level, smooth area for your veterinarian to work in (a grassy spot works well). Be sure your yearling has good manners for the pretranquilizer handling; veterinarians should not be subjected to potential injury from an unruly horse. Also, the more you can accustom your horse, in advance, to handling and restraint, the less stress he will experience during the gelding process.

One other thing you should do before the vet arrives is to study your horse thoroughly to determine what his "normal" appearance is. Look at his sheath, his legs, his eyes, and his facial expressions. Take his temperature, pulse, and respiration. Being familiar with your horse in an unstressed condition will help you monitor his progress in the postoperative period.

The gelding procedure may be performed while the horse is standing, lying on one side, or lying on his back, with the lateral recumbent position (on one side) most commonly used. A tranquilizer is usually administered to relax the horse, followed by a general anesthetic, which will make him lose consciousness. As the horse slowly collapses, care must be taken to ensure he does not injure his head or lose his balance and fall backwards. Once the horse is down, the anesthetic allows your veterinarian ten to twelve minutes for the procedure.

Restraint ropes are usually applied as a safeguard. The scrotal area is washed, and one or two incisions are made in the scrotum to remove the testicles. The spermatic cords are held in an emasculator for sixty seconds to crush and sever them.

The new gelding will get up on his own shortly after he comes out of the anesthesia. Since it takes about twenty to forty minutes for him to fully recover from the anesthesia, it is important that you put him in a safe, private place like a large sand arena or grassy paddock. Before you turn the horse out, apply petroleum jelly to the insides of his hind legs where fluids will later drip (photo 150). Hair can drop out and the skin can become irritated from the accumulation of wound drainage. The petroleum jelly not only protects the sparsely haired area from scalding but makes daily cleaning of the legs much easier for you and less painful for the horse.

As your young horse is recovering from the anesthesia in a safe facility, note if there is excessive bleeding or unusual behavior. Understandably, the gelding will be rather low in spirits and reluctant to move. If his attention and interest return an hour after surgery, that is a good sign.

When you feel he is coordinated enough to navigate, he may be turned out for quiet exercise with his usual pasturemates, providing they are not too rowdy. Although a horse's appetite may be somewhat weak at the first feeding after surgery, it should be voracious the next morning. After he has had a chance to digest his breakfast, you must begin his regimented exercise. The best preventative and treatment for swelling is a conscientious exercise program.

Hose your horse's legs and tail area each day after he exercises, being careful not to spray directly into the cavity (photo 151).

As long as the drainage from your horse's wound is watery and has an unoffensive odor, it is normal (drainage is largely comprised of serum and blood). If the incisions heal closed before two weeks or if there is a persistent bad smell, call your veterinarian immediately.

Because of surgical trauma, the gelding's sheath will swell (photo 152). Accumulation of fluids in that area is normal for four to five days. If the swelling becomes extreme or is accompanied by heat, you should notify your veterinarian. A swollen sheath may make it uncomfortable for your horse to urinate, so be sure to encourage normal urination by offering him fresh water at all times.

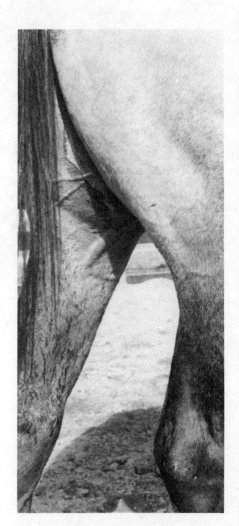

150. *The drainage from the incisions will drip down the hind legs and can cause scalding.*

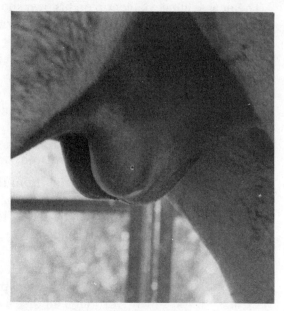

151. *Hosing once a day and applying petroleum jelly to the inside of the hind legs will minimize scalding.*

152. *The gelding's sheath will be swollen for several days following castration.*

Exercise

The following recommendations are designed for the small operation with one or two geldings per year. On large ranches, the procedures suggested here are labor-intensive and may be somewhat impractical. In those situations, a gelding can be turned out in a pasture to graze with his herdmates. The hope is that the horse will get adequate exercise. Frequently, this is true, but there is no guarantee.

Begin your horse's schedule with three fifteen-minute sessions each day for the first three days after surgery, two thirty-minute sessions for the next week, and then one sixty-minute session each day until healing is complete, which is usually about two weeks after surgery.

A combination of free longeing, ponying, and turnout will provide the required daily exercise. For this reason it is beneficial to teach your horse to longe before he is gelded. There is no sense in adding the extra stress of learning at a time when he is reluctant to move and perhaps not very attentive.

It is particularly important for your newly gelded horse that the footing in your round pen will not require him to pick up his feet any higher than necessary to keep from stumbling. Sand is preferred, both for safety and shock absorption, provided the sand has not become heavily compacted.

Free exercise is the least labor-intensive method of providing exercise for your horse, but it does not guarantee that he will exercise when he needs it the most. Often a new gelding will come out of his paddock or stall in the morning, barely able to move. After just five minutes of forced exercise, however, the incisions will reopen and drain, and the horse will seem instantly more comfortable and stride out much more freely.

Ponying is a very good way to provide vigorous exercise for the gelding. It takes up to several months for a young colt to physiologically realize he is a gelding, so if your pony horse is a mare be wary and wait to introduce the first ponying lesson until about the fifth or sixth day after gelding. By this time, the yearling has begun to move out more willingly, the exercise routine is something he has accepted, and he had graduated to the twice-a-day half-hour periods.

About ten days after gelding, you will alter the schedule to once a day for sixty minutes (actual exercise time, not counting grooming and saddling). Be sure to give him ample turnout time in addition to his regulated program.

As the gelding becomes conditioned from the consistent exercise, he may act rather feisty for the first few minutes of each lesson, so be careful. You may find it necessary to reinforce the leading lesson with a chain over his nose so that he remains light and very obedient to the pony horse's change in speed and direction. While ponying, review prompt halts and a few steps of backing.

Complications

There are some complications that can arise even with a routine castration. Swelling can spread down the hind legs in the body's sympathetic response to the swelling in the sheath area and/or, more probably, from the premature closing of the incisions and the inability of the area to drain. If drainage halts abruptly, you may need to have your veterinarian reopen one or both of the incisions. Occasionally, after recumbent surgery, horses will exhibit temporary facial paralysis from pressure on the facial nerve. This can be prevented by using a flat halter and a pad under the head during the gelding procedure.

Two weeks after your horse's surgery, from all outward appearances, you have a gelding. Past behavior patterns and residual hormones, however, tell the yearling otherwise. Use caution in turning the new gelding out with a group of mares, for example. He may learn a lesson the hard way.

Use good sense and caution when you introduce any new horse to a group. Let the horses get acquainted over safe fences, do not introduce them at feeding time, and be sure there are no traps where the young horse could get cornered. Observe the horse's behavior for a half hour so that you can separate the horses if necessary. (See Part Three, Chapter 11 for information on sheath cleaning.)

FILLIES AND THE ESTROUS CYCLE

Somewhere between the age of twelve and fifteen months, the filly begins to come into estrus (heat) periodically. The estrous cycle is the length of time from the first day of standing heat (estrus) in one cycle to the first day of estrus in the next cycle. (Note the difference in spelling to distinguish the entire estrous cycle from estrus, which is the heat period.) The average length of the estrous cycle is twenty-one to twenty-three days, with estrus lasting four to six days.

During estrus, the female shows interest in males, particularly stallions. Fillies in estrus may show any or all of the following signs:
- seeking the company of males or other herdmates if males are unavailable;
- raising the tail;
- spreading the hind legs;
- discharging mucous;
- urinating;
- "winking," which is repeated relaxing and contracting of the lips of the vulva with displaying of the clitoris;
- soliciting nibbling and chewing.

As a filly is coming into season (heat) or going out of season and while she is in diestrus (the non-estrus portion of her cycle), her behavior can be irritable and aggressive. It is not uncommon to see a filly striking, biting, squealing, and kicking as a response to other horses' seemingly inoffensive actions. In fact, what once may have been a pleasurable interaction of mutual grooming may now turn into an irritation for her.

Horses are seasonally polyestrous, that is, the females have viable heat cycles during a specific breeding season only. That season is determined somewhat by day length, but is basically early spring through early fall. During the winter months, a filly's ovaries are relatively inactive. At the beginning and the end of the breeding season and at the onset of puberty itself, a filly's estrous cycle can be very irregular. The length of time between cycles can be erratic and the heat periods can be extremely long, so-called "silent," or split.

Because of this variation in behavior, if you have a filly you must be flexible in your schedule and use precautions when working her with other horses. Some days it may be wiser to postpone a training session rather than get in a fight.

THE SPAYED FILLY

Although removing a filly's ovaries is not as commonly performed as gelding, there are circumstances in which spaying can be advantageous. For example, some breed registries allow a tentatively registered female to move up to permanent registration following an ovariectomy.

Certain physical problems can be alleviated with spaying. If a filly has developed dangerous behavior as a result of hormone imbalances resulting from an ovarian tumor, removing the ovaries can redeem her chance at a useful nonbreeding role. Mares with granulosa cell tumors usually display bad habits such as squealing, biting, kicking, and exhibiting stallionlike behavior. In 90 to 95 percent of the cases, surgical removal of the tumor and/or ovaries eliminates the undesirable behavior. Older mares who have developed cresty necks and voice changes will generally retain the characteristics after surgery.

Less dangerous fillies, but those with irritable, fussy, or silly periods every month may be regarded as a nuisance in terms of show, race, or ranch work. If a filly is valued, but not for breeding purposes, spaying may help her become a more solid performer.

A nonsurgical treatment for fillies with undesirable estral behavior is the administration of an oral synthetic progesterone, Regu-Mate. Progesterone is the calming female hormone responsible for maintenance of pregnancy. Regu-Mate inhibits the estrous cycle, which might provide temporary help during a prospective broodmare's show or race career.

There are currently three methods of removing the ovaries. Major abdominal surgery under general anesthesia is the most expensive method involving the longest recovery period, yet may be the only option available to horse owners in many locations. The surgeon makes a ventral midline incision from the umbilicus toward the udder, which gives him or her easy access to the ovaries. The surgeon has absolute hemorrhage control, which is essential when dealing with the ovary with a tumor, which is highly vascular. Major blood vessels are tied.

The horse usually remains in the hospital for observation for ten to twelve days, then is restricted to box-stall and/or paddock confinement for an additional thirty days. It is usually ninety days from the date of surgery until the mare can return to training. As with all major abdominal surgeries, there is always a risk of anesthesia and postoperative complications such as colic.

The flank approach to removing the ovaries is usually performed with the horse standing in stocks under the influence of a tranquilizer and local anesthetic. A four-inch incision is usually made in each flank to allow the surgeon easier access to each ovary. The ovaries are then removed with an emasculator, such as used in the gelding process, or with a chain-loop ecraseur, which is a surgical chain snare.

Recovery is quicker with this method than with abdominal surgery. The mare stays one day for observation in the hospital, then spends ten to fourteen days in stall and/or paddock confinement, and finally returns to work thirty days from the date of surgery. Generally the flank method provides few complications; however, it does yield minor scars.

The vaginal approach is the fastest, most inexpensive method of removing the ovaries, costing about one fourth as much as abdominal surgery. However, the vaginal approach requires a higher level of technical experience and may not be available in your area. Mares must be free from reproductive-tract infection and are routinely put on antibiotics before and after surgery. It is especially important when choosing this method to fast the filly for twenty-four to thirty-six hours prior to surgery to ensure minimal intestinal fill. Under the influence of a tranquilizer and local anesthetic, the filly is restrained in stocks. The surgeon enters through the vulva and makes a small incision in the vagina. He or she then severs the ovaries from their attachments with a chain loop ecraseur. No tying of vessels is required and no vaginal sutures are necessary. There is little trauma and jeopardy involved in the vaginal approach.

After surgery, the filly is usually kept standing in cross-ties for twenty-four to forty-eight hours, since lying down might allow protrusion of the intestine through the incision. During this time she should be periodically hand-walked for exercise. After three to four days in a box stall, she can be turned out in a paddock for a week, and then returned to work.

Determining when to spay a filly depends somewhat on the reason for the surgery and the chosen method. Abdominal surgery, which would be necessary for an individual with a large ovarian tumor, can be performed on a horse of any age. It is also an appropriate surgery for routine ovariectomy of the yearling as the longer recovery time would not interfere with a performance schedule. From a technical standpoint, both the vaginal and flank methods are best suited for a mare at least two to three years of age whose mature proportions allow the surgeon room to operate.

Spayed fillies no longer have estrous cycles and so do not exhibit estrous behavior. Otherwise there are no behavioral changes associated with an ovariectomy. Likewise, other than the absence of ovaries and the decrease in estrogen production, there are no physical changes. The mare's metabolism does not slow down; she does not become an easier keeper, and she does not gain weight more readily unless she is overfed. Neither do spayed fillies lose their feminine features. Your filly will look exactly as she did before surgery. More important, she will behave more consistently.

Removing a filly's ovaries is a permanent way of altering her estrous cycle and behavior. After careful consideration of your filly's breeding potential and intended use, you may find spaying is the answer to a management dilemma.

SIXTEEN

Evaluating Potential

THE MENTAL SET

Athletic ability can be both inherent and acquired, but a champion will more likely emerge from a horse that possesses special talents from birth. Observing the young horse as he interacts in a natural setting with other horses and as he responds to simple manmade tests can help you determine his potential for a particular sport. If several horses of the same age are compared, your interpretation is more useful. It is often evident shortly after birth whether a horse has inherited his sire and/or dam's aptitude for a particular event. A good pedigree doesn't ensure a high specialization aptitude, but it does increase the chances.

When evaluating a horse's mental set, begin by noting his sense of independence. A horse with an extraordinary physique and an insecure attitude will never reach full performance potential. A ranch horse, for example, needs to be comfortable dominating cattle and other horses, so must be confident. Horses high on the pecking order of a herd may be more difficult to train but may also show added brilliance during performance. A horse that is low in the hierarchy may need constant reward in order to develop a good opinion of himself. For demanding sports such as dressage, hunting, and eventing, you may find it easier to teach willing cooperation to an aggressive horse than to develop boldness in a meek individual.

Bonding between horses in herds or stables can present a problem. A horse with a low independence aptitude is often more concerned with the location of his stablemate than with his rider's cues and gives a halfhearted performance.

Youngsters who have been weaned without trauma, who have enjoyed the companionship of a variety of herdmates, and who have been handled as individuals from birth tend to be curious and

200

adventuresome. See how your yearling reacts when you lead him away from his herdmates (if this is not possible, observe him isolated in a safe pen separate from the others). You can expect him at first to call to his friends, but if he keeps calling and gets more and more anxious, you will know he lacks confidence. The insecure horse will be oblivious to attempts made by humans to communicate with him and may not pay attention to dangers and the limits of his confines. A horse with high self-esteem is usually quite independent. He will notice his separation from other horses, but will choose to investigate his new surroundings, remaining alert to things going on around him.

Even though domesticated horses depend on man for many of their needs, they still must take care of themselves. An individual with low self-preservation may stumble out of carelessness, panic and crash through a fence as if he didn't see it, or have trouble locating feed and water areas when he is put in new facilities. Self-preservation is a combination of alertness and "horse sense." Although it is not necessary for a horse to be suspicious of everything, it is the nature of the horse to be wary of unusual circumstances. That is what has helped him to survive for so many years. Certain family lines today have lost some natural instincts and tend to be overdomesticated.

To assess your horse's self-preservation, prepare a test pen. Place a few poles on the ground in a random fashion but where the horse must cross them, put a half-full bucket of water in the middle of the pen, and lay an empty paper feed sack on the ground. Put the horse in the pen and note his reactions. The secure horse with low self-preservation may stumble over the rails as if they posed no threat, might paw the bucket and tip it over, and will probably give little notice to the sack by shuffling over it or totally ignoring it. The insecure horse with low self-preservation may trot wildly and shy at the various objects or stand snorting in a corner with his tail raised. The survivor—the horse with high self-preservation—as he enters the pen may pause and survey the overall scene. Then he will probably look down at each rail as he carefully steps over it, sniff the water in the pail without touching the sides of the bucket, and inspect the sack to see if it might be harmful. Then he may stand calmly in a location that allows him to keep an eye on all of the objects.

Horses vary greatly in their tolerance for stress. While experience can increase an individual's tolerance, some horses are still susceptible to sensory overload in spite of their trainer's conditioning attempts. To test a horse's ability to sort out harmful stress, tie a bouquet of helium balloons on the rail of your horse's paddock or walk toward your horse's pen clapping your hands. Is he attentive or frightened?

Some horses are better than others in adapting to the pressures of domestication. A horse who has lived in one stall or in a particular pasture all of his life will probably find it hard to adapt to a new environment. A broad base of experience helps the horse to feel comfortable in a variety of circumstances. To gauge a horse's ability to adapt, put a pastured horse in a stall or a stalled horse in a pasture and watch his initial behavior the first few days. Does the horse immediately locate the source for food and water? Does he inspect the boundaries? Does he develop a defecation pattern similar to that in his last environment? Does he show signs of discomfort and distress by pawing, pacing, or weaving? Or does he stand at the pasture gate the majority of the time? How long does it take the horse to develop his new daily routines?

A horse who has been properly socialized with man has respect for but does not fear humans. Some individuals are "all horse" and a bit aloof, while others seem to prefer human interaction and companionship to that of their species. To see how certain horses react to people, approach a group of them in a pen. Staying the critical distance from them so that they settle down, note which ones face you with alert ears and which ones huddle with their rumps toward you. Turning a rump toward a human can indicate fear or lack of respect. Next, close the distance between you and the herd. Do those facing you turn and move away, hold their ground, or begin to step toward you? Watch the ears and head positions of the horses that have their rumps toward you. Which would be more likely to stand their ground and kick at an intruder and which would rather flee?

Another test for respect is to lead a horse on a slack line, trotting, then halting. If the horse crowds in front of you and steps on your toes, he lacks respect. If he swings to face you on a taut line, he may be fearful or arrogant. It is most productive to train a horse that is alert and slightly wary of his handler's moves.

An honest horse makes his intentions clear and has no secrets from his handler. Dishonest horses, on the other hand, are testy and just waiting for an opportunity to assert themselves. They are often very devious, never trying anything naughty if they know they will be caught. To test your horse's honesty, review a lesson he has supposedly been taught to do well, such as being unhaltered and turned loose. Be casual in your method, "baiting" the horse to do something wrong by letting your control of him lessen. The dishonest horse will sense the opportunity and may pull and wheel away prematurely. The honest horse will wait until your body language or voice tells him he can step away.

The alert, cooperative horse learns a new lesson in a relatively short period of time, while dull uncooperative horses may require many lessons and frequent reviews. Intelligence plus adaptability equals trainability. To test your horse's cooperation, choose a lesson he has not been taught, such as moving his hindquarters over while being tied to a post. Using similar aids as those used for the turn on the forehand, apply minimal cueing at first. Tip the horse's nose slightly toward you while applying intermittent pressure to the ribs in the approximate position of the rider's leg. The cooperative, alert horse often will perform this lesson correctly the first time from light finger pressure provided he has been set up in the proper position to comply with your aids. Uncooperative horses may require a convincing poke or a slap to get "unstuck."

See how many attempts you need to make before your horse understands what is being asked of him. Once he gets the message, does he begin to anticipate by swinging quickly away as your fingers approach his rib cage? The most desirable horse is one who learns quickly, requires minimal cuing, and responds to each cue with a separate reaction and without anticipation.

THE PHYSICAL SET

You should analyze your horse's conformation by assessing quality, substance, proper proportions, and correct angles. Quality is the overall merit of the horse. It is largely determined by genetics and is exhibited by well-defined features, smoothness of hair coat, and classy, elegant appearance. Substance can refer to depth and type of muscling, circumference and density of bone, roominess of joints, and size of hooves. Proportions dictate how well the horse's body will work as a unit.

Young horses often do not have desirable proportions but frequently grow into well-proportioned adults. The adult horse should have an approximately equal relationship between his leg length and girth depth, and his forehand should not be excessively heavier than his hindquarters. The yearling has proportionately longer legs, shallower heart girth, and undeveloped musculature. The adult's

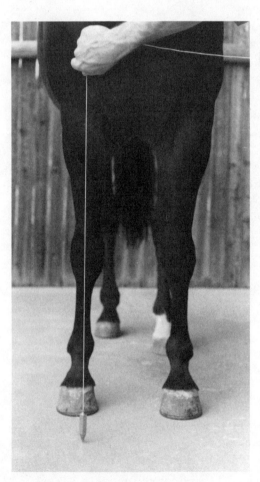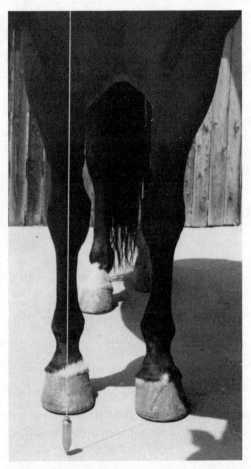

153. The slightly base-wide and toed-in front leg conformation that often causes paddling.

154. The very symmetric, straight bone alignment that results in efficient limb movement.

topline should conform to these ratios: the neck should be equal to or greater in length than the back and the rump should be equal to or greater than two-thirds the length of the back. Often the foal's hoof and pastern angles are much steeper than they will be as an adult. Correctness of angles, particularly of the limbs, gives a horse a better chance of reaching his potential while remaining sound (photos 153 and 154).

Besides evaluating conformation, you should look for other physical traits in your horse. Observing young sport horses at play in a pasture can separate those with the movement for dressage and those that are naturals at jumping, those that move like a pleasure horse and those that move like a reiner.

The **proprioceptive** sense allows a horse to rely on neuromuscular transmissions rather than entirely on sight to negotiate an obstacle. Strength in this sense is essential for hunter, jumpers, event horses, and trail horses. To test for it, you can free-jump or longe a long two-year-old over a small course. Natural talent and balance shows up as the horse goes over a fence the first time. Subsequent attempts might show that the horse is interested in improving his performance or that he is getting careless or bored. You can also lead or longe yearling hunter/jumper or trail prospects over ground rails or cavalletti on the lowest setting. Starting with the rails five feet apart, familiarize the youngster with the rails by leading him over them at the walk, and if he handles this well, at the trot. Compare the first, second, and third attempts. If the horse maintained composure through all three, hang on to him. If the horse does well the first time and his next attempts deteriorate, it is usually less desirable than if he lightly taps a rail initially but goes clean after that.

Coordination is closely coupled to the proprioceptive sense. A horse is well-coordinated if his body functions harmoniously when performing complex movements. To test coordination in a yearling, ask him to canter just as he approaches a one-foot jump in his longeing pen. If he canters without hesitation and on the correct lead, in addition to negotiating the jump without a knockdown, he is coordinated. Watch the way a prospect changes leads as he plays in the pasture. Look for a simultaneous, forward-moving flying lead change.

The flexibility of the horse's spine is especially important for dressage, jumping, and reining. A stiff horse can experience pain and/or damage when he is required to bend. A horse should be able to bend his head around to each shoulder and hold it there without distress and without moving his hindquarters. Holding a horse along a solid fence and trying this on each side will reveal muscular resistance.

A sensitive horse is more receptive to cues. Individuals with large eyes and nostrils and keen hearing perceive more subtle distinctions in their environment. The thin-skinned, sensitive horse has nerve endings that are close to the surface and readily receive stimuli from the rider's aids. To test certain horses' sensitivities, approach a group of them in a pasture. Which one is the first to hear you as you approach? Exert pressure on the horse's tendon above the fetlock. How much is necessary to get the horse to pick up his hoof? Examine the tongue. Is it pink, soft, and thin-skinned—or meaty and tough? Look at and feel the interdental space. Is the skin which covers the jawbone thin and tight, or thickened and coarse?

The ratio of fat to muscle in the growing horse should be very low. A young horse who is an easy keeper, or who has larger fat stores than his herdmates, may have a lower metabolic rate and/or a more efficient digestive system. Although this may appear to be an advantage from a management standpoint, an overweight youngster may turn into a lazy performer. A young horse who has the tendency to deposit fat in the neck or over the croup may have difficulty as an adult with freedom of movement in those areas.

The efficiency of the heart and lungs in providing oxygen and dispersing waste products during and after exercise changes dramatically as the horse matures. Rapid breathing and heart rate are characteristic of the young horse. It is valuable to compare your horse's rates with his herdmates'. Recovery rate is most important. Two-year-olds who don't respond to conditioning programs would be inappropriate candidates for racing or endurance events.

Strength, or an all-out effort exerted by a single contraction of a muscle, is necessary for most sport horses. Choose a young horse with the depth of muscle appropriate for the activity for which he is intended. The reining and cutting horse requires a powerful hindquarter to rapidly accelerate body mass from a standstill and to shift directions instantly. The competitive trail riding horse would be burdened with such a muscle mass, and is more successful with a longer, leaner muscle structure.

The horse's ability to balance his shifting weight, and later the rider's, during various maneuvers is necessary in all sports. Equilibrium is measured from side to side as well as from front to rear. As a horse loads in a trailer, he experiences a weight shift to his hindquarters and then to his forehand. This should happen smoothly and without exaggerated head and neck movements. Some horses have lateral balance problems. If a horse longes in a smooth arc with freedom of movement to the right, but stiffly and awkwardly to the left, he is not naturally balanced. Horses who routinely take the counter lead or canter disunited when longed in a twenty-meter circle have balance problems.

Toughness of joints and tendons is necessary for any work on deep, hard, or irregular surfaces. Hunters and event horses, especially, need this type of durability. Long, sloping pasterns may provide a more comfortable ride in some cases, but may indicate weak joints and tendons. Watch a prospect play in a deep sand pen, in a hard-surfaced paddock, or in a pasture with uneven terrain. In each case, watch the flexion and extension of the joints and the horse's overall freedom of movement.

Physical relaxation is necessary for maximum athletic achievement. A horse who does not release tension is working against himself during performance. Muscles are essentially involved in a give-and-take situation as they contract and relax. Each movement contains muscle groups that contract (agonists) and those that resist the contraction (antagonists). If a horse cannot relax he is creating unnecessary drag on one of his muscle groups because the reciprocal group cannot release its tension. Horses must breathe regularly throughout a workout and need to be relaxed in order to establish a rhythm. Watch a young horse in training on the longe line when he is asked to collect himself or extend; look for signs of tension when there is pressure exerted on the bit during long reining.

Ask a professional to help select a young horse, or challenge a home-raised prospect with a few of these simple tests and observations.

SEVENTEEN

Records and Journals

Keeping a written account of your young horse's health history, training results, and expenses is a solid business practice that can provide valuable information when the human memory slips.

Routine management practices such as vaccination, deworming, and farrier care are best recorded in chart form for easy retrieval. With training information you can combine chart and journal format. Sample forms and entries follow.

DEWORMING AND VACCINATION

Horse: **Zipper**   Date of Birth: **March 30**

Date	Product Used	Notes
4-28	Telmin	200 pounds body weight
6-04	Telmin	275 pounds body weight
6-17	Rhinomune	Right side of neck
6-30	4-Way	Left side of neck
7-07	Telmin Rhinomune	325 pounds body weight Right side of neck
7-22	Strongid P 4-Way	400 pounds body weight Left side of neck
8-26	Combatel	475 pounds body weight
9-29	Ivermectin	525 pound body weight
10-13	Flucine Rhinomune	Left side of neck Right side of neck
11-04	Anthelcide EQ	575 pounds body weight
12-16	Ivermectin	625 pounds body weight

FARRIER RECORD

Horse: **Zipper** Date of Birth: **March 30**

Date	Notes
5-15	Farrier said no need to rasp—good wear.
7-1	I held while farrier rasped lightly—good manners!
8-14	I held while farrier trimmed; not much correction. Will toe in slightly in front. Hind feet very straight.
8-26	Tied; used fly spray; picked up his feet.
11-04	Farrier trimmed while Zipper was tied—great!

VETERINARY NOTES

Horse: **Zipper** Date of Birth: **March 30**

Date	Notes
3-30	Iodine navel, enema.
7-30	Wean. Turn out with other mare and foal. No calling at all!
8-7	Hernia repair. Dr. Shideler. On the farm. Clamped tissue should fall off in 10 days.
8-14	Hernia repair successful.
11-16	Wound right front fetlock at inside. Clip; hot compress followed by cold hose.
11-17	Not lame but some puss. Use H_2O_2. Deep snow tonight will help keep cold.
11-18	Very little swelling and no infection apparent. Will keep an eye on it.

TRAINING JOURNAL

Horse: **Zipper**

March 5 Saddled and bridled at hitch rail. Was hobbled. Excellent manners. W-T-L both directions (30 min.) Tendency to lope at first. Tail tucked, but no buck. Good on whoa. Chews bit unless moving. Let him carry bridle in pen after lesson (10 min.) Clip in wash rack with large clippers while hobbled. Excellent.

March 6 Ponied. Needed to use chain over nose. Reviewed lesson in round pen for 15 minutes. He balked and pulled and reared several times, but finally got the hang of it. Ponied in and out of gates, around shop and yard and down canal road (30 min.) Excellent behavior. Carried snaffle—no chewing.

March 7 What a little star! Patient and well-mannered at the hitch rail. Good about bridling. Extremely cooperative and obedient on the longe line. Great progress on the three sizes of circles (35 min.) He carried the bit and wore a neck sweat. He's a pudgy one. Diet.

March 8 Ponied down the canal road (60 min.) Didn't spook at a thing. Neck sweat. Carried bridle.

March 11 Loaded in trailer next to Callie. Took on a four-mile ride—his first. From the feel of things, both rode very well. No manure. No nervousness. Groomed and turned out.

March 12 Saddled at hitch rail, bridled. Longed off halter with chain for 10–15 minutes. Good. Then hobbled in center of round pen while attaching driving ropes. Sacked him out gently with ropes around hind legs and under tail. Drove plow-style and circular-style at walk and trot (15 min.). Was very well-mannered, trusting, obedient, and sensible. What a wonderful little horse. (Someday he is going to cut loose with a bucking spree though!)

March 20 He couldn't wait to hop in the trailer next to Ms. Zinger. We three went to Lory Park and did a four-mile loop. I hobbled Zipper at the trailer and left him while Zinger and I rode around the parking lot. He hopped around a little and tested the hobbles. He ponied really well except for when he saw "The Rock" (the big orange one standing out in the middle of nowhere). He pulled back violently once and then stood attentively. We walked up to inspect. On the way back, he was very honest and didn't spook (2 hours).

March 21 Loaded into the trailer solo. I hauled him to Taft Hill Horse Farm, where I unloaded him on Taft Hill Road. He was very trusting of me and stayed right by my side as I led him around the various new sights. He wasn't even scared of the goat! Some lumber piles gave him the most concern. I longed him for about 30 minutes, then groomed him in the cross-ties in the barn, then put him in a stall while we worked Dale's horses. He was a real gentleman. And he loaded really well for the return trip!

March 25 Fitted with a driving rig, and drove English and Danish style (30 min.) Was driving lesson 2 and he never made a false move!

March 26 Clipped fetlocks. Was hobbled at wash rack. Very good.

May 17 Without tranquilizer, but with hobbles and twitch, he got dental care for a snaffle mouth. He was very well-behaved and got compliments from the vet on his disposition.

July Three one- to two-hour ponying sessions with Zinger. One on canal road and two at Lory Park. Very good sessions all.

August 12 Saddle, bridle, longe (30 min.), weight in stirrup.

August 13 Saddle, bridle, drive (30 min.) Excellent. No withers in sight, so another diet!

August 18 Saddled, bridled, and put in round pen for one hour.

August 25 Drive (20 min.)—good.

August 26 Pony down canal road and to dead end (2 hours). Good. But he stops and balks when defecating. Must work on that.

APPENDIX

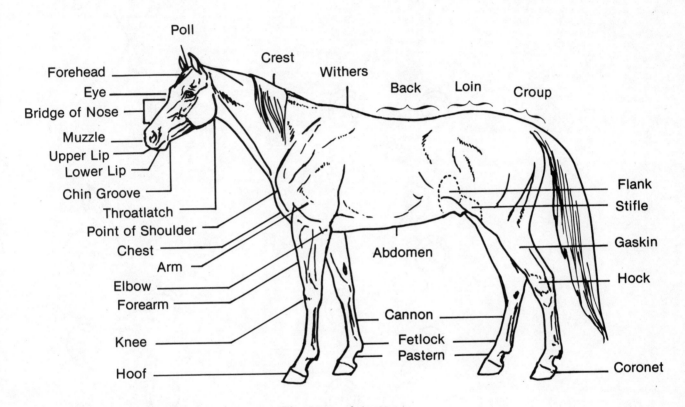

Poll

Crest

Withers

Back   Loin   Croup

Forehead

Eye

Bridge of Nose

Muzzle

Upper Lip

Lower Lip

Chin Groove

Throatlatch

Point of Shoulder

Chest

Arm

Elbow

Forearm

Knee

Hoof

Abdomen

Cannon

Fetlock

Pastern

Flank

Stifle

Gaskin

Hock

Coronet

The Parts of the Horse

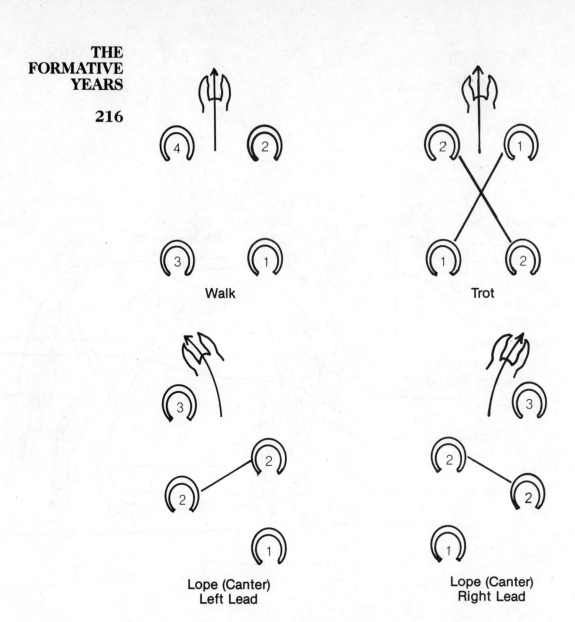

The Gaits of the Horse

TRAINING CHECKLISTS

Suckling Foal
Catching
Haltering
Unhaltering
Leading with dam
Leading alone
  Walk
  Halt
  Turn in large circle
Tying to inner tube
Grooming
Manners for hoof care while held
Load in stock trailer with dam

Weanling
All preceding lessons
Manners for hoof care while tied
Move over while tied
In-hand
  Walk
  Trot
  Halt
  Turn to left
  Turn to right
Stand for veterinary treatment
Introduce chain (if necessary)
Introduce twitch (if necessary)

Yearling
All preceding lessons
In-hand
  Back
  Turn on the hindquarters
  Turn on the forehand
  Halt on the long line
  Sidepass

Obstacles
  Walk over tarp, plastic, paper sacks
  Ditch
  Cement
  Puddle, creek
  Ground poles
Load, haul, and unload in a two-horse trailer
Restraint
  Scotch hobble
  Front leg strap
  Hobbles
Sacking Out
  Blanket
  Ropes
  Slicker
Clipping
  Legs
  Bridle path
Pulling mane (if necessary)
Bathing
Cleaning sheath or udder
Ponying

The Long Yearling
Longeing
  Walk
  Trot
  Halt

The Two-Year-Old
All preceding lessons
Fit with bridle or bosal
Longeing
  Canter/lope on both leads
  Extension and collection
  Add side reins

Surcingle
Saddle
Driving/Long-Reining
  English/Western plow-style
  English/Western circular
  Danish circular
    Walk
    Trot

Canter/lope
Halt
Back
Turn left
Turn right
Figure-eight at walk
Figure-eight at trot

Nutrient Requirements and Ration Guidelines

Foal: **Birth to 3 months of age   16% Protein Required**
Alfalfa hay (13–19% Protein) or Pasture.
Mare's milk. No individual grain ration.
1:1 Ca:P Trace-Mineral Salt Block or Loose Mineral.

Foal: **4 Months of Age   16% Protein Required**
Alfalfa hay (13–19% Protein) or Pasture.
Grain: .5–.75 pounds per 100 pounds of body weight
per day. (Approximately 1–2 pounds per day for
most foals.)
1:1 Ca:P Trace-Mineral Salt Block or Loose Mineral.

Weanling: **4 to 12 months of age   14.5% Protein Required**
Alfalfa hay with 1:2 Ca:P Trace-Mineral Salt Block or
Loose Mineral (if alfalfa hay tests high in calcium)
          or
Alfalfa/grass hay or pasture with 1:1 Ca:P
Trace-Mineral Salt Block or Loose Mineral.
Grain: 1–1.5 pounds per 100 pounds of body weight
per day. (Approximately 2–8 pounds per day for
most weanlings.)

Yearling: **12 to 24 months of age   12% Protein Required**
Same forages and minerals as weanling ration.
Grain: .5–1 pounds per 100 pounds of body weight
per day. (Approximately 2–8 pounds per day for
most yearlings.)

Sample Immunization* and Deworming Plan
Foal Born April 1, 1987

1987

May	1	Deworm
	15	Rhinopneumonitis and Influenza
June	1	Deworm
		Western Equine Encephalomyelitis
		Eastern Equine Encephalomyelitis
		Tetanus Toxoid
	15	Rhino & Flu
July	1	Deworm, WEE, EEE, and Tet
August	1	Deworm
	7	Wean
September	1	Deworm including for bots
	15	Rhino & Flu
October	15	Deworm
December	1	Deworm incl/bots

1988

January	15	Deworm
March	1	Deworm incl/bots
April	15	Deworm
		4-Way (WEE, EE, Tet, & Flu) plus Rhino
June	15	Deworm
August	15	Deworm
October	15	Deworm incl/bots
December	15	Deworm incl/bots

1989

February	15	Deworm incl/bots
April	15	Deworm
		4-Way plus Rhino

*Frequency of influenza and rhinopneumonitis vaccine dependent on exposure to other horses. Confer with your veterinarian about the necessity to vaccinate for strangles, rabies, and VEE.

CLASSIFICATION OF DEWORMERS

Class	Chemical	Brand name

BENZIMADAZOLES
Effective against strongyles and oxyuris.
High margin of safety.

	*mebendazole	Telmin
	thiabendazole	Equivet TZ
		Omnizole
		Equizole
	*cambendazole	CamVet
	fenbendazole	Panacur
	oxybendazole	Anthelcide EQ
	oxfendazole	Benzelmin

*also effective against ascarids

ORGANOPHOSPHATES
Effective against bots, ascarids, oxyuris.
Potentially toxic for foals under four months of age. Can cause diarrhea and colic and abortion in pregnant mares past midgestation.

	*dichlorvos	Equigard
		Equigel
	trichlorfon	Combot

*also effective against strongyles

PHENOTHIAZINE/PIPERAZINE
Effective against strongyles/ascarids.

CARBAMATES
Effective against strongyles, ascarids, tapeworms.

	pyrantel pamoate	Strongid T
	pyrantel tartrate	Banminth
		Strongoid

IVERMECTIN
Effective against strongyles, ascarids, oxyuris, and bots. Safe for
foals.

ivermectin   Eqvalan
                                              Zimectrin

COMBINATIONS
Effective against strongyles, ascarids, oxyuris, and bots.

piperazine + phenothiazine +
trichlorfon   Dyrex TF
Caution: Trichlorfon is an organophosphate.

piperazine + phenothiazine +
carbon disulfide   Parvex Plus
Caution: carbon disulfide can cause diarrhea and/or colic.

thiabendazole + piperazine   Equizole A
Effective against strongyles, ascarids and oxyuris. Safe for foals.

GROWTH RATE OF THE LIGHT HORSE*
(From *Feeding and Care of the Horse* by Lon Lewis, Lea & Febiger.)

Age (months)	% of Mature	
	Weight	Height at Withers
birth	8–9	61–64
1	16–18	66–68
3	27–29	75–77
6	45–47	83–86
9	56–58	89–91
12	65–69	91–93
18	78–83	94–96
24	87–92	96–98
30	93–97	97–99
36	95–99	98–100
48	98–100	99–100

*The larger horse (1300 lbs or 590 kgs) will be on the low end, and the smaller horse (700 lbs or 318 kgs), on the upper end of the range given. Draft horses' rate of growth is slower than the values given, e.g., 50% of mature weight is attained at 1 year, 75% at 2, and 90% at 3 years of age; and ponies' growth rate is faster (55% is attained at 6 months, 75% at 1 year, and 84% at 18 months of age). Body weight, height at withers, and circumference of front cannon bones are lowly heritable at birth but are highly heritable by 18 months of age (0.90, 0.88, and 0.77, respectively). Colts are heavier and taller at birth and have bigger cannon bones than fillies, and the differences increase with time. All three of these parameters are smaller in foals born to mares less than 7 or older than 12 years old than in foals born to mares between these ages.

RANGES OF
GROWTH PLATE CLOSURE TIMES IN
EQUINE THORACIC LIMBS*

Scapula
  Proximal** 36+ mo.
  Distal 9–18 mos.

Humerus
  Proximal 26–42 mos.
  Distal 11–34 mos.

Radius
  Proximal 11–25 mos.
  Distal 22–42 mos.

Ulna
  Proximal 27–42 mos.
  Distal 2–12 mos.
  (some up to 4 yrs.)

Third Metacarpal Bone
  Proximal Before Birth
  Distal 6–18 mos.

Proximal Phalanx
  Proximal 6–15 mos.
  Distal Before Birth to 1 mo.

Middle Phalanx
  Proximal 6–15 mos.
  Distal Before Birth to 1 wk.

Distal Phalanx
  Proximal Before Birth

*From Lea & Febiger STASHAK #C3738-N: Adams' Lameness in Horses, Fourth Edition, 1986.
**Ossification center

GLOSSARY

accommodation   The self-adjustment of the lens of the eye for focusing on objects at various distances.

adaptation   Changing so that behavior will conform to new circumstances; in vision, the power that the eye has of adjusting to variations in light.

acuity   Keenness or sharpness of vision

aid   The means by which a trainer communicates with the horse.
   natural aids   Mind, voice, hands, legs, body (weight, seat, back).
   artificial aids   Crop, whip, spurs, chain.

articular   of or pertaining to a joint.

attitude   A temporary behavior reflecting specific conditions.

back   A two-beat diagonal gait in reverse.

back-splice   A means of turning the strands of a rope back on themselves to prevent the end of the rope from fraying. It results in an increase in diameter of the rope.

barn sour   Herd-bound; a bad habit that may result in a horse bolting back to the barn or to his herdmates.

bars (mouth)   The bony, flesh-covered space between the incisors and molars where the bit lies. Also called the interdental space.

bell boots   Protective boots, usually of rubber, that encircle the coronary band and the bulbs of a horse's heels.

binocular   Using both eyes at the same time.

bit guard   A rubber or leather ring which lies between the horse's cheek and the bit ring or shank to prevent skin pinching

bitting rig   A surcingle with rings through which driving lines may pass or to which reins may be attached.

bosal   A rawhide noseband of varying thicknesses used in training horses. It works on the principles of balance, weight, and pressure.

bot block   A hard but porous synthetic black "stone" similar to a grill stone used to clean restaurant grills. The uniformly abrasive surface will remove bot eggs from the horse's hair. The block can be "sharpened" by drawing it across a hard edge.

bowline   A nonslip knot that will untie even if tightened very snugly. Used in restraint procedures.

breakover   The moment in a horse's stride between landing and takeoff.

canter   The English term for a three-beat gait that is very similar to a Western lope.

cavalletti Ground rails suspended between two large wooden Xs, designed to provide three different heights for working horses. A very small jump.

cavesson A leather noseband.

bridle cavesson The standard noseband with many English bridles. It encourages a horse to keep his mouth closed.

longeing cavesson A headstall with a weighted leather or nylon noseband with metal rings for attachment of the longe line.

cold-blooded Having ancestors that trace to heavy war horses and draft breeds. Characteristics might include more substance of bone, thick skin, heavy hair coat, shaggy fetlocks, and lower red-blood-cell and hemoglobin values.

colic Abdominal pain cause by gas, impaction, intestinal damage from parasites, etc.

collection A state of equilibrium where the horse is energized, alert, and ready to respond to the requests of the trainer.

colt A young uncastrated male horse four years and younger.

conditioning The art and science of preparing a horse mentally and physically for the demands of an event.

creep feeder A grain feeder with openings small enough to only admit the muzzle of the foal; a portion of the facilities that only admit foal-sized animals to enter.

crown knot The star configuration that is the beginning of a back-splice in a three-stranded rope.

cue A signal or composite of trainer aids that is designed to elicit certain behavior in a horse.

curb A type of English or Western bit that has shanks and therefore works on the principle of leverage action. A curb may have a solid or jointed mouthpiece.

curb strap A leather strap which is affixed to the bit below the reins and lies in the chin groove. When used with a curb bit, it creates pressure on the chin groove from the leverage action of the shanks. When used with a snaffle, it prevents the snaffle from being pulled through the horse's mouth.

dally To take a wrap with a rope around the saddle horn of a Western saddle.

dam The mother of a horse.

distal Remote or farther from a particular point of reference.

disunited Cantering or loping on different leads front and hind. Also known as cross-cantering.

dock The flesh and bone portion of the tail.

dressage French for training. A highly organized, progressive system of maneuvers designed to teach a horse suppleness, balance, and fluidity of movement in addition to obedience.

dropped noseband A piece of tack, usually made of leather, designed to allow the nosepiece to be located lower than a cavesson. Worn over the bit, it enhances sensitivity to the bit by positioning it on the bars and encouraging salivation. It is also used to encourage a horse to keep his mouth closed.

electrolyte A substance that when in solution has an electrical charge. It is important in many bodily processes such as digestive metabolism and muscle-tissue functions.

encephalomyelitis Inflammation of the brain and spinal cord; "sleeping sickness."

engagement The use of the horse's back and hindquarters to create energy and impulsion to forward movement. An engaged horse has a rounded topline, a dropped croup, flexed abdominals, and an elevated head and neck.

epiphysis The growth plates at the ends of long bones.

equus The genus of the horse; the species of the modern horse is equus caballus.

extension A lowering of a horse's frame with a lengthening of his stride.

extinction Removal of a pleasant reinforcement to discourage the behavior it follows.

exudates matter discharged in drops as through pores (sweat) or from an incision (drainage).

evasion Avoidance of an aid; for example, the behavior of a horse that overflexes or gets "behind the bit" to keep from accepting contact with the bit.

eye splice A loop which is back-spliced into the end of a rope.

fiador A knotted throatlatch used in conjunction with a bosal, browband headstall, and horsehair reins. The knots of the fiador are the hackamore, the fiador, and the sheet bend.

filly A young female horse four years of age and younger.

Flehmen response A behavior in reaction to a smell in which the horse raises his head and curls back his upper lip.

flexion A characteristic of a supple and collected horse.

  lateral flexion Side-to-side arcing or bending characteristic of a horse doing circular work.

  vertical flexion An engagement of the entire body—abdomen, hindquarters, back, neck, and head. Often mistakenly associated with "head set." Also called longitudinal flexion.

flying lead change In the canter or lope, the change from one lead to another without changing gait.

foal A young male or female horse under a year old.

gait Sequence of foot movements, such as walk or trot.

gelding A castrated male horse.

gregarious Social; living in herds.

ground-driving The western version of long-reining.

ground tie Having a horse stand still when the lead rope is dropped on the ground.

habituation Repeated exposure to a stimulus, thus decreasing the horse's response to it.

hand A measurement used in calculating a horse's height at the withers. A hand equals four inches.

hobble To restrain the horse by securing his front legs together. The restraint used for hobbling.

hot-blooded Having ancestors that trace to Thoroughbreds or Arabians. Characteristics might include fineness of bone, thin skin, fine hair coat, absence of long hair on fetlocks, and higher red-blood-cell and hemoglobin values.

hypermotile Increased activity such as in the intestine.

impaction A type of colic or abdominal pain caused by low gut motility, obstruction, or constipation.

imprinting The rapid learning in a young horse's first field of vision that reinforces species behavior.

impulsion The desire and energy of forward movement.

influenza A viral infection involving the respiratory tract.

instinct Inborn, intrinsic knowledge and behavior.

intelligence Ability to survive or adapt to man's world.

intermittent pressure Application and release of an aid (in contrast to steady pressure).

intramuscular Deep into muscle tissue.

jaquima Spanish for hackamore. Actually indicates the entire rig—bosal, headstall, fiador, horsehair reins, and **mecate**.

jog A slow Western trot.

lariat Lasso; a twenty-foot rope, usually about ½-inch in diameter, made of synthetic or natural fibers. Most lariats have a hondo, or permanent loop, at one end.

latent learning A type of learning that has been assimilated but has yet to be demonstrated.

lateral Generally indicates "to the side" (a sidepass is a lateral movement); lateral aids are all applied on one particular side of the horse;

also an anatomical term usually meaning toward the outside as opposed to toward the midline.

lead A specific footfall pattern at the canter or lope in which the legs on the inside of a circle reach farther forward than the legs on the outside. Working to the right, the horse's right foreleg and right hind leg reach farther forward than do his left legs. If a horse is loping in a circle to the right on the left lead, he is said to be on the wrong lead, or he may be counter-cantering.

legume Any of a group of plants of the pea family that store nitrogen in the soil; alfalfa is an example.

longeing Working a horse on a line around the trainer.

longitudinal flexion Bending that takes place in the vertical plane (as opposed to lateral flexion, which takes place in the horizontal plane).

long-reining The English term for ground-driving. Working the bridled horse on a pair of long reins in front of and around the handler.

long trot Moving a horse at a trot other than a jog.

long yearling A horse in the fall of its yearling year; usually a yearling eighteen months of age.

lope A three-beat gait with an initiating hind leg followed by a diagonal pair including the leading hind leg and finally the leading foreleg.

mecate A 22-foot horse-hair rope, 3/8- to 3/4-inch in diameter, that is fastened to a bosal to make reins and a lead.

modeling Observational learning or mimicry.

monocular Using one eye.

nasal turbinates Passageways from the nostrils to the lungs.

negative reinforcement Removing an aversive stimulus to encourage the behavior it follows.

nomadic Wandering or roaming.

panic snap A snap with a quick-release collar; often used in horse trailers.

pecking order Caste system or social rank.

pivot A crisp, prompt turn on the hindquarters.

poll The junction of the vertebrae with the skull; an area of great sensitivity and flexion.

pony horse The mount that is ridden while the trainer leads another horse from him.

ponying Leading a horse while riding another horse.

positive reinforcement Reward; giving something pleasant to encourage the behavior it follows.

power of association The ability to link an action and a reaction; a stimulus and a response. The key to training horses since they will try to avoid mistakes and earn reward.

proprioceptive sense Awareness of body parts and movement.

proximal Nearest or closer to a particular point of reference (as opposed to distal).

punishment Administering something unpleasant to discourage the behavior it follows.

rabies A viral infection that affects the nervous system.

rein-back Back; a two-beat diagonal gait in reverse.

reinforcement Strengthening an association with primary reinforcers, (inherent) such as feed or rest, or secondary reinforcers (paired with primary and learned) such as praise or a pat.

resistance Reluctance or refusal to yield.

restraint Preventing a horse from acting or advancing by psychological, mechanical, or chemical means.

rhinopneumonitis An upper respiratory infection of young horses that can also cause abortion in pregnant mares.

rounding Engagement of the muscles, characterized by an arched back, a dropped croup, hind legs well under the body, flexed abdominals, and an elevated head and neck.

sacking out Gentling (usually by accustoming to flapping objects).

Scotch hobble To tie up the hind leg of a horse; the restraint used for Scotch hobbling.

sebum The semiliquid, greasy secretion of the sebaceous glands.

septicemia Blood poisoning by microorganisms and/or their toxic products.

shank A lead rope or "stud" chain. Also, the arm extending from the mouthpiece of a curb bit where the reins attach. Pressure on the reins exerts leverage.

shaping The progressive development of the form of a movement; the reinforcement of successive approximations to a desired behavior.

side reins Reins, usually with an elastic component, that are attached to a bitting rig or saddle while a horse is longed.

snaffle A bit with no shanks that works on direct pressure. The mouthpiece may be solid or jointed.

splint boots Protective covering worn around the cannon of the front legs to prevent injury.

splints A term commonly applied to inflammation of the attachment of the splint bone to the cannon; older cases of splints are identified as bony enlargements at the splint bone.

strangles Equine distemper caused by *streptococcus equi* bacteria; highly infectious and characterized by inflammation of the respiratory mucous membranes.

stress tolerance level   The point at which a horse can no longer absorb stress (noise, exercise, or trauma) and failure results.

substance   Of solid quality as in dense bone or large body size.

suckling   The nursing foal.

sullen   Sulking, resentful, withdrawn.

supple   Flexible.

surcingle   A piece of training tack that encircles the horse's heart girth. It can be used when longeing or driving and acquaints the horse with saddling.

tack   Horse equipment or gear.

temperament   The general consistency with which a horse behaves.

terrets   Rings on the surcingle (or any harness) through which the reins pass.

tetanus   An infectious disease of the nervous system caused by a bacterial toxin and commonly associated with puncture wounds.

thrush   A disease of the hoof, often associated with unsanitary conditions, which causes decomposition of the frog and other hoof structures.

titer   Concentration.

transition   The upward or downward change between gaits and maneuvers.

trot   A two-beat diagonal gait.

turn on the forehand   A maneuver in which the horse's hindquarters rotate around his forehand.

turn on the haunches (hindquarters)   A maneuver in which the horses horse's forehand rotates around his hind end.

twitch   A means of restraint. A nose twitch is often a wooden handle with a loop of chain that is applied to the horse's upper lip. A shoulder twitch is applied by grabbing skin at the horse's shoulder and rolling in around the knuckles.

tying up   A form of metabolic muscle stiffness caused from irregularity in feed and work schedules.

vertical   In the vertical plane, that is, perpendicular to the horizon.

vices   Undesirable behavior patterns that emerge as a result of domestication, confinement, or improper management.

voice command   A natural training aid. It must be consistent in word used, tone, volume, and inflection.

walk   A four-beat gait combining lateral and diagonal components. If the right hind leg is the first to move, it is followed by the right front, then the left hind, and finally the left front.

war bridle A device also called a "come-along" that exerts poll pressure on a horse.

weaning Separating the foal from its dam (usually done at four to six months of age).

weanling The young horse of either sex who has been separated from the dam but has not yet turned one year old.

whip To finish the end of a rope by wrapping it with cord; an artificial training aid.

wither rope For use with the problem puller, this long cotton rope encircles the horse's heart girth, then passes between the front legs and through the halter, and then is tied higher and shorter than the halter's lead rope is tied. When the horse pulls, pressure is exerted on the thorax rather than on the head.

yearling A young horse of either sex from January 1 to December 31 of the year following its birth.

SUPPLEMENTAL READING

The Art of Long Reining, Sylvia Stanier, J. A. Allen, London, 1972.

*The Art of Lungeing, Sylvia Stanier, J. A. Allen, London, 1976.

The Body Language of Horses, Ainslie and Ledbetter, Morrow, New York, 1980.

Cavalletti, Reiner Klimke, J. A. Allen, London, 1973.

Feeding and Care of the Horse, Lon D. Lewis, Lea & Febiger, Philadelphia, 1982.

Grooming To Win, Susan E. Harris, Charles Scribners Sons, New York, 1977.

Handbook of Livestock Management Techniques, R. A. Battaglia and V. B. Mayrose, Burgess Publishing, Minneapolis, 1981.

The Horse, Evans, Hintz, and Van Vleck, W. H. Freeman Co., San Francisco, 1977.

Horses, J. Warren Evans, W. H. Freeman Co., San Francisco, 1981.

Horse Behavior, George H. Waring, Noyes, New Jersey, 1983.

Horseshoeing Theory and Hoof Care, L. Emery, Jim Miller, and Nyles Van Hoosen, D.V.M., Lea & Febiger, Philadelphia, 1977.

The Horse, Structure and Movement, Smythe and Goody, J. A. Allen, London, 1971.

How to Make Cowboy Horse Gear, Bruce Grant, Cornell Maritime Press, Maryland, 1956.

How Horses Learn, Jeanna C. Fiske, Stephen Greene Press, Vermont, 1979.

The Illustrated Veterinary Encyclopedia for Horsemen, Equine Research, Texas, 1975.

Lameness in Horses, Ted Stashak, ed., 4th Ed., Lea & Febiger, Philadelphia, 1986.

Knots and Splices, Percy W. Blandford, Arc Books, New York, 1968.

Leather Braiding, Bruce Grant, Cornell Maritime Press, Maryland, 1961.

*The Mind of the Horse, L. H. Smythe, J. A. Allen, London, 1972.

Nutrient Requirements of Horses, National Research Council, Printing and Publishing Office, National Academy of Science, Washington, D.C., 5th Ed., 1986.

*Available from Breakthrough Publications, Millwood, New York 10510.   **233**

Restraint of Animals, John Leahy and Pat Barrow, Cornell Campus Store, New York, 1953.

Training the Young Horse and Pony, The Pony Club, British Horse Society, England, 1964.

Western Horse Behavior and Training, Robert W. Miller, Doubleday/Dolphin, New York, 1975.

Index

235

236

238

Remodeling, bone, 190
Respect for humans, 202
Respiration rate, 144-45
Restraint
  defined, 49
  of weanling, 49-57
  of yearling, 73-84
Ringworm, 164
Ropes
  lead, 28, 29
  rump, 36, 37
  sisal rope lines, 124
  wither, 50, 82-84
Roughages, 169
Roundworm (ascarid)
    infestation, 147, 148
Routines, daily, 9-11
Rubber, stable, 42
Rubber, curry, 42
Rubber grooming mitt, 42
Rump rope, 36, 37

Sacking out, 14, 84-87
Saddle, introducing, 118-21
Safety
  in long-reining, 124
  in restraint of yearling, 76
  in training, 26-27
Salivary reflex, 115
Scotch hobble, 76-79
Self-preservation, 201
Sensitivity, 7
  assessing, 206
Serum protein livels, 149
Sesamoids, proximal, 189
Sex, temperament and, 6
Shank, 24
  chain, 50, 54-57
Shaping, 17-18
Shipping, physical stress of, 183
Shoeing schedules, 138-39
  See also Hoof care
Shoulder twitch, 54
Shying, 5
  during longeing, 109

Side reins, introducing, 121-22
Sideline, 81-82
Side-pass, 62, 63, 64
Sisal rope lines, 124
Sleep positions, 9-10
Slow-wave sleep, 10
Smegma, removal of, 161-62
Smell, communication through, 8
Snaffle bit, 110
  behavior in, 117
  selecting, 112-17
Socialization, 3-4, 177, 202
Soybean meal, 170
Spayed filly, 197-99
Spina prominens chain, 26
Splint bones, 186, 188
Splint boots, 98, 99
Splints, 188
Spoons, 117
Stable rubber, 42
Stallion, 191
Stalls, 174
Startle response, 5
Stiffness during longeing, 109
Strap, front leg, 73, 79-80
Strength, evaluating, 206
Stress, 179-90
  immunological, 183
  from longeing, 98-99
  mechanical, 184-90
  metabolic, 183
  physical, 183
  psychological, 180-83
  tolerance for, 84-87, 179, 202
Substance, assessing, 203-4
Sucking reflex, 25, 142
Suckling foal. See Foal; Foal,
    training of suckling
Surcingle, introducing, 118-21
Sweat, neck, 90
"Sweet feed" grain mixes, 170
Swimming, 178

Tack
  introducing horse to, 110-22

  safety of, 26-27
Tail care, 164
Tail protection, 165
Tail rubbing, 161-64
Teeth
  care of, 151-57
  groups of, 151
  signs of problems, 151-53
Temperament, 6-7
Temperature, mean resting, 143
Tendons, 186, 207
Terrain, mechanical stress and
    surface of, 185
Testosterone, 191
Tests, blood, 148-50
Thredworms (strongyloides), 148
Thrush, 158
Tolerance for stress, 84-87, 179,
    202
Tongue, 110-11
Tools, grooming, 42, 43
Trailering
  physical stress of ride, 183
  of suckling foal, 47-48
  unloading, 72
  of yearling, 69-72
Trainer
  attitude of, 22
  characteristics of successful,
    133
  hands, bit selection and, 114
  working with, 140,41
Training
  checklists, 217-18
  confrontation, 180
  facilities, 27
  of foal, 23, 28-48, 49-57
  interval, 179
  journal, 210-11
  of long yearling, 96-109
  longeing, 96-109
  principles and guidelines,
    21-27
    body language and voice
    commands, 8, 16, 23-25, 40

240